Gimme Shelter – A Democracy If We Can Keep It

Contents

Published in the United States by Swpubl Publishing

ISBN: **9798870566306**

ACKNOWLEDGMENTS

I acknowledge that my experiences of the 60s moved me beyond just a front lawn, a white picket fence, and a Chevrolet to look forward to. Being a free and tortured soul inspired much of this book. The brightness of the hippy, New Frontier, and rock eras blended into the horror of death and the heroes of that time, leading me to this day. I am privileged to have met some of the heroes of Democracy, from RFK to Eldridge Cleaver. What a life it has been.

Introduction

-As Americans, we face a serious political threat to our democracy. This book aims to inform readers about this threat and its causes clearly and concisely. The historical and current factors leading to this situation are urgent, especially with the upcoming mid-term election. Democracy is at risk of being replaced by a fascist-style regime in our federal government. To prevent this, we must understand how the Trump administration is gaining power and what it means for our future. This book provides brief but relevant insights to help readers understand this complex dynamic. While this writing may not appeal to everyone, it is a necessary effort. The book is based on research and personal opinion, allowing you to draw informed conclusions. I do not apologize for revealing some facts and arguments that may be shocking to some, but I feel compelled to do so. An update has been added since its previous publication.

The sources of the information are provided as they appear in their original form.

Introduction to the update
Democracy at a Crossroads: Trump, Putin, and the Crisis of Institutions

The United States faces a critical crossroads today, where the continuation of democratic institutions cannot be assumed. Challenges from authoritarian regimes are rising both overseas and domestically, reshaping the global landscape and destabilizing domestic governance. Russia's imperial ambitions under Vladimir Putin threaten NATO and European security. At the same time, Donald Trump's leadership approach and political goals undermine the constitutional rule of law in the U.S. This introduction explores how these forces interact, starting with the geopolitical contest involving NATO, then examining Trump's neglect of democratic norms, his use of tariffs as economic strategy, and the broader authoritarian plan outlined by Project 2025. The discussion also looks at how surveillance technologies may facilitate authoritarian control and draws parallels with historical crises like Vietnam and war. Collectively, these developments pose a serious challenge to whether the American experiment in self-governance can survive.

I. Geopolitical Context: Russia, NATO, and Authoritarian Influence

Ukraine's sovereignty remains a key part of Russia's broader strategic goals. Once part of the USSR, Ukraine is not just a symbolic target but also a gateway for Putin's aim of restoring Russian influence. His long-term goal extends beyond Ukraine, focusing on weakening and ultimately dismantling NATO. A divided NATO would leave Europe exposed, weakening the security structure that has kept the continent stable since World War II. European independence also acts as a protective barrier for the West.

Putin's influence goes beyond Europe. During Trump's presidency, Russian leverage crept into the White House, shaping stories and deepening divisions. Putin's and Trump's carefully built 'tough-guy' images hide deep insecurities, since real strength depends on competence and legitimacy, not coercion. His ability to exploit Western weaknesses highlights the danger of domestic leaders ignoring their own democratic institutions.

II. The Rule of Law and the Crisis of American Democracy

At the core of democracy is the idea that law overrides personal loyalty. As Judge Luttig explains, in a democracy, law is the supreme authority. Man is not. Trump's approach to governing challenges this principle by treating institutions as tools for personal loyalty. His dealings with the judiciary exemplify this pattern, turning constitutional processes into exchanges of favor and gratitude.

The consequences of such an outlook are serious. If leaders can ignore court orders without facing consequences, the rule of law breaks down. In these moments, institutions need to stand firm through strong enforcement. Agents like the U.S. Marshals may be forced to act even against protective services, reaffirming that no one is above the law. Democracy relies on this firm defense of institutional independence.

III. Economic Policy: Tariffs, Inflation, and Wealth Transfer

Trump's economic plan relies heavily on tariffs, which act as hidden taxes on lower- and middle-income groups. Although framed as a nationalist approach, tariffs have historically weakened economies by increasing consumer prices and limiting growth.

The consequences extend beyond economic inefficiency. Tariffs shift wealth upward, moving the tax burden from corporations and the wealthy to ordinary families. Inflationary pressures artificially inflate asset values, benefiting elites while reducing living standards for most people. Comparing Argentina and Turkey demonstrates how manipulated economic systems create the illusion of prosperity for the wealthy while pushing entire populations into hardship. In this way, tariffs are not just poor policies—they serve as tools for a significant transfer of wealth, carried out openly and justified as patriotic protectionism.

IV. Historical Parallels: Vietnam, and Contemporary Conflicts

Historical memory is crucial in shaping public opinion and political behavior. During the Vietnam War, loyalty to the country was often linked to unwavering support for military actions. Dissent was portrayed as betrayal, even when policy mistakes were clear.

A similar pattern continues today in debates over U.S. support for Israel. Historically connected to Holocaust remembrance and Cold War tactics, Israel has often been seen as beyond criticism in American political discussions. However, recent conflicts, especially in Gaza, reveal troubling similarities between past oppression and current state violence. Domestically, Trump capitalizes on fears of rising costs and immigration, framing complex issues as existential threats. These narratives resemble Cold War-era distortions, where fear and misinformation replaced nuanced debate.

V. Project 2025: A Blueprint for Authoritarian Governance

One of the biggest threats to American democracy is Project 2025, created by the Heritage Foundation as a plan for Trump's possible return to power. Its proposals aim not just for small reforms but for a complete overhaul of the government into a centralized executive system.

Labor and the Economy: The plan seeks to dismantle worker protections, restrict union organizing, and eliminate public sector unions. These measures would weaken one of the last defenses against corporate power, reducing labor's influence on national policy.

Health Care and Social Policy: Provisions include removing caps on drug prices, setting lifetime limits on Medicaid, and cutting programs like Head Start. These actions could limit healthcare access, harm early childhood education, and increase inequality.

Immigration and Sovereignty: The agenda advocates for militarized immigration enforcement, including the deployment of active-duty military, and calls for dismantling the Department of Homeland Security. These policies embody an authoritarian view of sovereignty rooted in coercion and exclusion.

Climate, Economy, and Governance: Other suggestions

include abolishing the Federal Reserve, reestablishing a gold-backed currency, cutting funding for renewable energy, and bringing the federal bureaucracy under direct presidential control. These measures align with the 'unitary executive' theory, which aims to eliminate checks and balances and concentrate extraordinary power in one individual.

VI. Technology and Surveillance

The rise of surveillance technologies heightens the risks of authoritarianism. Palantir Technologies emphasizes the dangers of secretive, privately developed systems embedded into government functions. Criticisms include facilitating mass data collection, predictive policing, and covert partnerships with agencies like ICE.

When such technologies operate without transparency, they become tools for unchecked surveillance and control. In the context of Project 2025, the merging of political authoritarianism with technological surveillance would pose a serious threat to civil liberties and democratic accountability.

VII. Trump's Leadership Style and Institutional Breakdown

Trump's career path shows a pattern of inherited privilege, repeated financial failures, and reliance on spectacle.

His reality TV career projected competence where there was none, solidifying an image that later helped him gain political power.

In his first term, experienced officials acted as some safeguards against chaos. However, a second term is mostly filled with loyalists who lack institutional knowledge or independence. This leads to dysfunction and vulnerability, where government becomes weakened and crises are likely. Authoritarian movements flourish in such unstable environments.

Conclusion: Defending Democracy

The threats facing American democracy are diverse: authoritarian aggression abroad, erosion of institutions at home, economic tactics that shift wealth upward, surveillance tools that threaten privacy, and political plans aimed at increasing executive power. The crisis extends beyond traditional partisan boundaries. What's really at risk is not just certain policies but the core survival of democracy itself. Trump's movement thrives on loyalty, fear, and spectacle rather than rational debate or institutional accountability.

The choice for the United States is straightforward. Either institutions and citizens come together to protect democracy, or they risk seeing it disintegrate, piece by piece, leaving only authoritarian rule.

Gimme Shelter -- The End Of Democracy As We Know It. A republic if we can keep it.

Gimme Shelter, the end of the 60s

In the spring of 1969, Keith Richards, the iconic guitarist of The Rolling Stones, sat in a dimly lit apartment, strumming his acoustic guitar and lost in thought as raindrops streaked down the window. Richards reflected on that moment in his memoir, "Life." "There was this incredible storm over London," he recollected, "so I got into that mode, just looking at all these people running like hell. It was just a terrible day, and the idea came to me… My thought was storms on other people's minds, not mine. It just happened in the moment." (The Rolling Stones Gimme Shelter- Pop Go The Sixties 1969).

The storm triggered the creation of The Rolling Stones' legendary song, "Gimme Shelter." As chaos engulfed the world around him, Richards crafted the melody that would soon become a symbol of the end of an era. The world was shifting; the idealism of the 1960s was fading, and the song captured those turbulent times, and the present day. The Melody: The haunting opening lines of "Gimme Shelter" mirror the brewing upheaval both in the world and American society:

"Oh, a storm is threat'n

My very life today

 If I don't get some shelter,

Oh yeah, I'm gonna fade away."

This lyrical storm marked a sharp shift from the flower power and peace movements that defined the decade. Author Ian Rankin observed, "It reflected the times, the end of the 60s and the hippy idealism... The world seemed to be going to hell, reflected in the lyrics and the sound." As if on cue, the San Francisco "Summer of Love" celebration of peace, love, wonder, flowers, Weed, and LSD, and all the creativity that came with it, took a turn toward the end of that summer. In contrast, George Harrison came to visit Golden Gate Park and the Haight-Ashbury area. The police became relentless with the young hip types visiting and living there. Those who came to see the beautiful hippie phenomenon saw the place take a turn for the worse, with harsh drugs, drug pushers, ordinary homelessness, and criminals coming to take advantage of the stoned kids and the kindness of the hippies. The Summer of Love was soon overshadowed by the darkness of war, despair, and meanness as it seeped into the culture.

If only today, during these 2000s, had something, anything, that could temper what Mary Trump, Donald Trump's niece, called Trump's life philosophy in her first book on the family. In particular "Cruelty Is The Point." The cruelty she is addressing involves taking children from parents, taking workers from fields and sending them to the gulag, the cruelty of taking medical help from the elderly, and food from the mouths of children. Cruelty for Uncle Donald is an expression of toughness and masculinity.

The early '60s, once a time of hope and optimism, had become an era marked by the assassination of all of our leaders, the brutal horror of the Vietnam War, riots, protests, police beating and killing protesters, 1800 bombings in 1970s alone, and rampant political chaos. The joyfully stoned Woodstock Festival followed the first rock festival, Newport '69, celebrated for its countercultural spirit, was later overshadowed by the

Altamont, California, concert tragedy, where choosing the Hells Angels as security guards led to death and violence. The Rolling Stones, known as the rebels of the era, embodied the spirit of change and chaos, signaling the end of the promise of the '60s with "Gimme Shelter." Fast forward to today in the 2020s, and the gloom and anger are even stronger. The happiness and idealism that marked the '60s have faded somewhere between then and now. The 60s were difficult but democracy was never threatened. Sometimes, optimism emerges from the ashes, only to be replaced by lurking darkness. Amid fears about a controversial 2024 election, the country faces issues of manipulation, division, violence, a major threat to democracy, and widespread racism. The scars from a terrible disease remain. Covid killed over a million people, and leadership suggested bleach as a cure amid its incompetence. The optimism of the past is hard to find, and shadows now cast an even broader darkness. The lyrics of "Gimme Shelter" reflect a bleak view of the world, contrasting with the song's rhythmic core.

> Ooh, see, the fire is sweepin'
> Our streets today Burns
> like a red coal carpet
> Mad bull lost its way
> Rape, murder, it's just a shot away

It's just a shot away.

The 1960s witnessed a series of transformative musical and cultural shifts. The Beatles, once leaders of American youth culture, pioneered change with songs like "Tomorrow Never Knows," steeped in Eastern thought and the influence of LSD, questioning the very foundation of American reality. The counterculture, led by artists like Bob Dylan, rejected uber-conformity, paving the way for a new era of progress and change for the better. Yet the times became brutal and punishing. Maybe it is just the human condition and its realistic manifestation.

Those bright 60s moments of respect, progress, and humor during the Kennedy Presidency—such as ideas like the Peace Corps, civil rights, poverty eradication, and wise decision-making—were suddenly ended on the streets of Dallas by assassination. However, Congress passed civil rights laws aimed at ending discrimination against groups other than white middle-class Christians, only to be overshadowed by the assassination of Martin Luther King. The era was then consumed by a relentless tunnel of hell and violence in Vietnam, protests, and the killing of demonstrators. A brief return to hope happened when RFK ran for President in 1968, but was cut short when the candidate was shot and killed in a kitchen in L.A.—marking the abrupt end of optimism for progress in that decade. America's divisions deepened further with police riots outside the 68 Democratic convention in Chicago, the senseless beating of hundreds of anti-war protesters, and the fatal shooting of student protesters at Kent State University, with no legal repercussions—completely accepted by war supporters. ("We Were Not Playing Games": Transnational Moral Policing in 1970s Vancouver, 2021.)

Today, the American political system, dominated by supporters of "MAGA," short for the "Make America Great Again" slogan of the Trump campaign, may also serve as a slogan for putting our freedoms at risk. Before this last presidential election of Donald Trump 2, an opinion piece from the Washington Post states this succinctly:

"Like people on a riverboat, we have long known there is a waterfall ahead but assume we will somehow find our way to shore before we go over the edge. But now the actions required to get us to shore are looking harder and harder, if not downright impossible. The magical-thinking phase is ending. Barring some miracle, Trump will soon be the presumptive Republican nominee for president. When that happens, there will be a swift and dramatic shift in the political power dynamic in his favor." (Kagan, Washington Post, Sept 2023)

Progress and rights won in the 60s

The civil rights movement and the Vietnam War

protests were two of the most critical social and political pillars of the 1960s and 1970s in the United States. They challenged the status quo by demanding racial equality under the law, social justice, and changes in both foreign and domestic policies. They also influenced and inspired each other in various ways, such as the civil rights movement, which revealed the hypocrisy of the U.S. government's claim to promote democracy and freedom abroad while denying these rights to millions of its own citizens at home. Many civil rights activists viewed the Vietnam War as a continuation of colonial oppression and exploitation of people of color. They explained this exploitation as the use of poor minority youth as expendable, the first to be sent into the Vietnam jungle to be killed by Viet Cong fighters.

In contrast, white political leaders highlighted that the military provided opportunities to develop new skills and access educational opportunities for minorities. Many anti-war protesters also supported the civil rights movement. They criticized the war's diversion of federal funds from domestic programs and the disproportionate number of Black war casualties compared to the total number of soldiers killed in Vietnam. War protests drew attention to the war's costs, the moral and legal implications of the U.S. intervention in a sovereign nation. It soon became apparent that this was due to

President Johnson's ego problem. He could not cope with being the first president to withdraw from a war.
(Nation. https://nmaahc.si.edu/explore/stories/civil-rights-and-vietnam-war-era).

The civil rights leader Martin Luther King Jr. was one of the most prominent and influential figures who connected the two movements. He publicly opposed the war on moral grounds, condemning it as a "tragic adventure" that was "Taking the black young men who had been crippled by our society, sending them eight thousand miles away to guarantee liberties in Southeast Asia which they had not found in southwest Georgia and East Harlem." (Nations.https://www.history.com/topics/vietnam-war/vietnam-war-protests) He also organized and participated in anti-war rallies and demonstrations.

The Black Power movement emerged in the late 1960s as a radical and militant branch of the civil rights movement, closely linked to the anti-war movement. Many Black Power activists, such as those in the Black Panther Party, criticized the U.S. government for waging a racist and imperialist war against the Vietnamese people and called for solidarity with the liberation struggles of oppressed peoples worldwide. Some Black Power groups also adopted the name and symbols of the Mau Mau. The Mau Mau revolutionary organization fought against British colonial rule in Kenya during the 1950s to express resistance to the U.S. military and political establishment. Taking action through street protests helped end the war and put civil rights at the forefront of the national agenda, leading to essential changes.

The times are a-changin'

The question remains: where are we as a country today? Who the hell are we really? The optimism that once fueled change during the watershed 1960s in American history has yet to return. The hope of that time is hardly a memory, and political gloom hangs over everything. So, we start with the present. In this critical moment, looking back at the past is essential. This gloom threatens Democracy, possibly even ending it in the West.

"Gimme Shelter," although released in 1969, embodies the darker facets of this decade. The song reflects the chaos and fear caused by rampant racism, issues around immigration, voting rights, the fear of homosexuality, book burning, censoring accurate American history, and the looming threat of violence against anyone not supporting the MAGA agenda, with the reality of a future dictator of America. It's all around us, and no one is surprised. America sleepwalked into the authoritarian rule of Trump, eyes wide open.

In contrast to the darkness of the 1960s, it was also a time of significant progress and hope, particularly within the civil rights movement.

President Johnson, succeeding Kennedy, championed and signed several landmark civil rights bills into law, including the Civil Rights Act of 1964 and the Voting Rights Act of 1965. These legislative achievements marked a turning point in the fight against racial segregation and discrimination, embodying the decade's spirit and striving toward equality and justice.

The 1960s experienced a mix of hope and darkness, with each affecting the other. The civil rights movement was a symbol of hope also facing the dark realities of racism and violence. The Vietnam War angered many, leading them to protest. These issues caused people to question their traditional values and shift the culture. It may have been the intense protests that finally ended the war in Vietnam.

A Republic If We Can Save It

We tend to believe that our democratic heritage automatically shields us from threats like autocracy, but this is a false sense of security. The precedent set by the Founders requires us to study history to understand the roots of tyranny and consider how to respond appropriately. Today, Americans are no wiser than Europeans who faced the rise of Fascism, Nazism, or communism in the twentieth century. One thing we do have is the ability to learn from their experiences. Now is an ideal time to do so. (Timothy Snyder, Tyranny)

Benjamin Franklin –A Republic If You Can Keep it

In his closing speech to the convention, Franklin said: "…when you assemble a number of men to have the advantage of their joint wisdom, you inevitably assemble with those men, all their prejudices, their passions, their errors of opinion, their local interests, and their selfish views."

"A lady asked Dr. Benjamin Franklin, "Well, Doctor,

what have we got, a republic or a monarchy?" "A republic," replied the Doctor, "if you can keep it."

The first time this quote appeared in print was in 1906 in the *American Historical Review*. James McHenry, a Maryland delegate to the constitutional convention, noted it. It reflected the fear among many of the delegates regarding the fragility of Democracy.

The fact that the American Republic has lasted nearly two hundred and fifty years is extraordinary. Many republics quickly fall into dictatorship, even if they keep the title. He realized that the form of government he helped establish was vulnerable and could easily slip into tyranny. He and his colleagues had a classical education and understood that this had happened centuries earlier in Greece and Rome. (Walter Isaacson, in Benjamin Franklin: An American Life)

Our Republic is a Democracy.

Many Americans who are transforming their country into a monarchy or an authoritarian-style regime try to promote the idea that the United States is a "constitutional republic" rather than a democracy. They believe that voting and majority rule are forms of ignorant tyranny. Some use the term "mob rule" for dramatic effect. They argue that a "Constitutional Republic" is the way to have a wise dictator make all decisions, knowing better than the majority. Interestingly, Plato deeply disliked the Athenian democratic government that sentenced his teacher, Socrates, to death in 399 BC. In his "Republic," he compares democracy to a ship with a mutinous crew. Perhaps MAGA is akin to the DNA of Plato returning through karma, seeking revenge.

An article on this comes from the Atlantic magazine." (George Thomas, **"America Is a Republic, Not a Democracy' Is a Dangerous—And Wrong—Argument"** Atlantic, November 2, 2020).

Professor Thomas says the American experiment has been about harmonizing democratic and republican models, two "popular forms of government," each of which "drew its legitimacy from the people and depended on rule by the people."

The key difference was the role of representatives in replacing the need to gather everyone at one place and time. That would have caused a lot of chaos. The idea of government by the people, including both a democracy and a republic, was clear when the Constitution was drafted and ratified," Thomas said. "It also overlooks how we understand democracy today." Allowing a sustained minority rule at the national level is not part of our constitutional design but a distortion of it," Professor Thomas explains.

One way to understand that idea was articulated by

Thomas Jefferson himself in 1816 when he wrote:

"We may say with truth and meaning that governments are more or less republican as they have more or less of the element of popular election and control in their composition."I take from this **Republic and Democracy to be controlled by popular election by a majority.**"

America has been a Democracy for almost 250 years, *the Constitution guaranteeing freedoms that could not be known under a king, dictator, or authoritarian rule*, thus getting away from institutionalized non-reality and, for example, the church controlling the state through the fear of hell for disobeying the church leader as a control mechanism. The definition of freedom, then, is to follow your own lifestyle and say and do what you want, even if critical of the political or religious leader. Democracy gives us the freedom to practice odd sexual behavior, speak freely, and do most things, *but not to take away others' freedoms*, put others at violent risk, or take property not belonging to us. Republicans wish for the freedom to take away others' freedoms. As one candidate put it, another's freedom is no one else's business, and it is "weird" to complain about others' freedoms.

We had this democracy up to Trump without question; since then, it has been under threat. We fought wars, and many died, to preserve this democracy and these freedoms. Many of these freedoms have come slowly in this republic. For the first time in history, a time comes to test the hypothesis: "A Republic, if you can keep it." Likewise, a democracy, if we can keep it.

"The Constitution establishes a federal democratic republic form of government. That is, we have an indivisible union of 50 sovereign States. It is a democracy because people govern themselves."

(Our American Government | Congressman James E. Clyburn, https://clyburn.house.gov › Youth Activities)

The following is added:

To be clear, besides being a representative democracy, the United States is also a constitutional democracy, where courts limit the democratic will to some extent. Therefore, the United States is also a constitutional republic. In fact, the United States can be described as a constitutional federal representative democracy.

However, where one word is used, with all the simplification that this entails, "democracy" and "republic" both apply. In fact, since direct democracy—again, a government in which all or most laws are made through direct popular vote—would be impractical given the number and complexity of laws that nearly any state or national government is expected to pass, it's not surprising that the term "representative" is often left out. Practically speaking, representative democracy is the only form of democracy that exists at any state or national level. (State and even national referenda are sometimes used, but only for a very small portion of the state's or nation's lawmaking.)" (The Volokh Conspiracy, Mostly law professors, 1/19/2022)

An authoritarian who would rule by whim, who would destroy the rule of law and institutions that have served to keep the U.S. a Democracy for all, an authoritarian who is successful at attacking those constitutional freedoms and taking away the freedom to choose any religion or no religion, or the freedom to read any book or say what you wish, must be resisted by the majority for the Republic to be kept intact.

The 45th (and 47th) president took it upon himself to seek complete control by accumulating power through a "MAGA" minority in America—those who felt left behind or took offense to some of the long-sought freedoms of others, like civil rights. The culture wars have become real, no matter how incredible it may seem. Violence has increasingly entered American politics as a tool to gain political control, starting with a defeated president and the J6 insurrection of 2020. Those who *refused to partake in the "big lie"* that Trump was really elected President in 2020 are heroes for standing up to it. And those accused of participating in the "rigged" election—whether volunteers attacked for counting votes or secretaries of state who did not change votes in favor of #45—who faced threats against themselves or their families' lives, are also heroes.

Worse, most of the GOP has accepted Trump's claim

that America is under 'mob rule' democracy, and the main problem for the Republican Party is that it has no real platform or policy. It's a party with no reason to exist except to tear down America and hand it over to their leader to turn into a kingdom where everyone is white and Christian. It has become the party focused on destroying its opposition or any liberal American ideas—any small difference, from dress to sexual orientation, any thinking or behavior outside of the 1950s mold—mother, flag, apple pie, and especially the white race. The primary goal of this party is to ensure the white race's dominance. The white race must be the only community present in our neighborhoods or when they run for office. No race other than white should enter the United States to live or dream of a better life, hoping to become what makes us American. Race is not only about skin color but also about speech, accent, culture, celebrations, arts, rituals, and many harmful stereotypes. For example, Black children suspended from school because of their hair clearly carries racial overtones.

Maga ideology, ridding America of freedom

The "MAGA" movement enjoys popularity among Republicans who have gained considerable influence in recent years. They have pursued this path because their core values struggle to gain traction among voters in most elections. Much of the electorate views MAGA issues as toxic and illegitimate. Some of these issues include:

- Attempts to restrict or censor certain books they do not like

- Opposition to abortion

- Revisionism in historical education, particularly concerning racial discrimination (polls in most states indicate that most voters trust teachers to make these judgments)

- Resistance to same-sex marriage and various forms of LGBTQ discrimination (Odd sex may seem strange, but who cares)

- Advocacy for permitless carry of firearms and the elimination of background checks (87% unpopular in America

- Calls to end Social Security and Medicare (Senators Mike Lee, John Thune, and other Republicans)

- "Maga" Republicans are aware that these issues are divisive and unpopular yet reflect their cultural preferences. Implementing their policies would *infringe upon the freedoms of others*, making them highly anti-. Democratic and unconstitutional if codified.

Over the years, these Republicans have tried to control

these issues and impose their views on others, ultimately aiming to dictate their neighbors' lives. This contrasts with the 250-year American tradition of fighting for and defending individual freedoms, even those we might disagree with, as the GOP's current path seems to aim at restricting them, taking away the liberty that America fought many wars and lost many lives to protect.

The Kragan opinion piece referenced earlier in this writing from The Washington Post suggests that there is an American self-delusion about the election of a dictator rich with imagined possibilities. The liberal American voter believes that America is immune to the authoritarian manner in which Trump seeks. That the country will heal and return to sanity with midterms. Such hopeful speculation has allowed us to drift along passively, conducting business as usual, taking no dramatic action to change course, in the hope and expectation that something will happen.

Until now, traditional Republicans and conservatives have enjoyed relative freedom to express anti-Trump sentiments, speak openly and positively about alternative candidates, and voice criticisms of Trump's behavior, past and present. Donors who find Trump distasteful have been free to contribute money to support his opponents. Establishment Republicans have made no secret of their hope that Trump would be convicted of his crimes and thus removed from the equation without them having to oppose him directly. Instead, he has immunity as the 47th president of the US. (Kagan, A

Trump Dictatorship Is Increasingly Inevitable, Washington Post, Nov 30, 2023).

Project 2025 (It only gets worse)

A quick summary of Project 2025 follows:

Labor and Unions

- **Public sector unions face survival threats:** Project 2025 suggests banning them altogether, claiming they're incompatible with constitutional governance.

- **Reversing Davis-Bacon wage protections** and ending

project labor agreements would weaken private sector unions.

- **Union organizing** would be harder: card check elections would be eliminated, and decertification would be easier.

Health Care

- **Medicare reforms** would repeal the $35 insulin cap and the $2,000 out-of-pocket drug cost ceiling.

- **Medicaid** could face lifetime coverage caps—some suggest a 36-month limit—which would affect millions of low-income Americans.

- **Drug price negotiations** would be eliminated, reversing recent efforts to lower costs.

Education

- **Department of Education** would be dismantled, shifting control to states and promoting school choice.

- **Head Start** would be eliminated, affecting over 800,000 children in poverty.

- **Student loan forgiveness** programs would be scrapped, including Public Service Loan Forgiveness and income-driven repayment plans.

Immigration

- **Department of Homeland Security** would be dismantled and immigration agencies consolidated.

- **Military involvement** in border enforcement would be expanded, including arrests in sensitive locations like schools and churches.

- **Fees for immigrants** would increase, with fast-track options for higher payments.

Economy and Federal Reserve

- **Massive tax cuts** are proposed for both corporations and individuals.

- **Abolishing the Federal Reserve, Trump is working on that, and returning to a gold-backed currency is floated as an option.**

Climate and Environment

- **Renewable energy funding** will be slashed.

- **NOAA** would be downsized for its role in climate change research.

- **Environmental regulations** would be rolled back to favor fossil fuels.

Reproductive Rights

- **Abortion access** would be severely restricted: Mifepristone could be banned or limited to seven weeks of pregnancy.

- **States requiring abortion coverage** in insurance could lose up to 10% of their Medicaid funding. This is already part of a trump promoted bill as passed.

- **A "pro-life task force"** would replace the current Reproductive Healthcare Access Task Force.

Gender Identity and Civil Rights

- **HHS would declare** that "men and women are biological realities," rejecting gender identity protections.

- **Title IX protections** for LGBTQ+ students could be rolled back.

- **DEI programs** eliminated across federal agencies.

Unitary Executive Theory

- **Presidential control** over the entire federal bureaucracy would be expanded. Control over all other branches of government.

- **Civil service protections** would be removed, allowing mass replacement of career officials with political appointees loyal to trump.

- **Independent agencies** like the DOJ would be brought under direct presidential authority.

"Project 2025" is a plan to reshape the U.S. federal government to support the agenda of second Trump term, point blank. The director of this project is Paul Dans (see: Website ww.project2025.org). *An update to this section has been added in this book.*

Project 2025 is a plan to structure the executive branch of the U.S. federal government in the event of a Republican victory in the 2024 United States presidential election. *Shah, Areeba (2023-09-05). ("Dark" right-wing network recruits MAGA "army" to replace 50K federal workers Trump plans to purge". Salon. 2023-09-24.)*

The project aims to recruit thousands of conservatives to Washington, D.C., to replace existing federal civil service workers it labels as the "deep state," whom they believe are trying to "get" Trump. The deep state is seen as a paranoid belief that Steve Bannon relayed to Trump and the GOP to advance Donald Trump's agenda and policies.

Upon the inauguration of Trump in 2025, the plan entails a takeover of the executive branch under a maximalist version of the "unitary executive theory," a theory proposing the President of the United States has absolute power over the executive branch. Call it a dictatorship, call it authoritarian. The plan's development is led by the Heritage Foundation, a conservative U.S. organization, in association with other organizations, including the Conservative Partnership Institute and the Center for Renewing America. (Hirsh, September 9, 2023, "Inside the Next Republican Revolution." *Politico*.)

It envisions widespread changes in the federal government's and its agencies' role, mainly concerning economic and social policy. The Washington Post reported that the plan includes immediately invoking the Insurrection Act to *deploy the military for domestic law enforcement and directing the U.S. Department of Justice to pursue Trump's adversaries.* In November 2023, *The Washington Post* reported that deploying the military for domestic law enforcement under the Insurrection Act would be an "immediate priority" upon the second Trump inauguration in 2025, with any expected protest across the country. Jeffrey Clark, a Trump co-defendant in the Georgia election racketeering prosecution, and an unnamed co-conspirator in the federal prosecution of Trump for alleged election obstruction, are leading that aspect of the plan. The plan also includes directing the Justice Department to pursue those whom Trump considers disloyal and those he considers his political adversaries. (*Isaac Arnsdorf; Josh Dawsey; Devlin Barrett November 5, 2023 "Trump and allies plot revenge, Justice Department control in a second term." The Washington Post.) The DOJ is now pursuing those disloyal in any way.*

America, at the moment, has a new Speaker of the House chosen in a manner reminiscent of an under-the-radar selection process. It turns out that he played a significant role in attempting to deny President Biden's confirmation in 2020. He was part of the conspiracy to convince the American populace that the presidential election was fraudulent and that Trump had emerged the victor. Many individuals who were part of this conspiracy have begun admitting to the falsehood and are cooperating with authorities in exchange for leniency in their legal consequences. (Bradwater, New York Times, October 25, 2023).

Interestingly, this new speaker replaced the original speaker, who struck a deal with Democrats to govern the nation. He dared to negotiate with Democrats for funding to keep the country running. Yet this new speaker also negotiated with the Democrats to keep the government running. Maga's objective is to allow no money to be spent to keep the nation going. The original speaker said:

"I don't understand why anybody votes against bringing the idea and having the debate," McCarthy told reporters. "This is a whole new concept of individuals that just want to burn the whole place down." (Guardian, Sept. 21, 2023)

Meanwhile, Democrats seek ways to allocate funds already set aside for infrastructure development and to enhance Social Security so that our elderly can spend their final years with some certainty of food and health.

This Project 2025 plan sounds like the same threat that Trump expresses out loud through his speeches and tirades on our judicial system. He also shows little fear of the four legal jurisdictions that have indicted him, maybe because of the promise of Project 2025.

During an interview with Univision, the Spanish network, he declared that he would "weaponize" the DOJ and FBI to indict and jail all of his enemies, anyone who opposes him now or opposed him during his presidency. In private, the former President has told advisers and friends in recent months that he wants the Department Of Justice to investigate former Trump officials and allies who have become critical of his time in office, according to people who have talked to him and spoke on the condition of anonymity to describe private conversations.

Trump has also talked of prosecuting officials at the FBI and Justice Department, a person familiar with the matter said. Trump told Maegan Vazquez of Univision he would weaponize the FBI and DOJ against his enemies. (Washington Post, November 10, 2023)

In another interview, Trump gave similar answers. He would carry out a deportation operation aimed at removing more than 11 million people from the country. He would be willing to build migrant detention camps, currently in progress, and deploy the U.S. military, both at the border and inland, to capture non-white immigrants. He would allow red states to monitor women's pregnancies and prosecute those who violate abortion bans. He would withhold funds allocated by Congress at his discretion, according to top advisers. He fires any U.S. Attorney who doesn't follow his orders to prosecute someone, breaking with independent law enforcement that dates back to America's founding. He granted 1500 pardons to those accused of attacking the U.S. Capitol on Jan. 6, 2021, more than 800 of whom have pleaded guilty or been convicted by a jury. He might not come to the aid of an attacked ally in Europe or Asia if he feels that country isn't paying enough for its defense. That could mean breaking from NATO and allowing Putin to expand his territory. He is gutting the U.S. civil service, through an incompetent doge agency, deploying the National Guard to

American cities as he sees fit, closing the White House pandemic-preparedness office, and staffing his administration with followers who support his false claim that the 2020 election was stolen from him.

In public, Trump has promised to appoint a special prosecutor to "go after" Biden and his family. The president frequently alleges corruption against them, without any supporting evidence I could find. When he criticizes judges and court officials in his way, they often receive numerous death threats. Many election officials he criticized faced hostile crowds in front of their homes, and some had to leave their house, which is a subtle way of intimidating those who might oppose him within the legal system and institutions—marking a significant step toward fascism.

His associates working on "Project 2025" have drafted plans to disregard 50 years of shielding criminal prosecutions from *political* considerations, thereby facilitating Trump's ability to direct Justice Department actions. Such ideas are not only counter to democracy, but one would think dangerous and unconstitutional.

During his interview with Univision, Trump also sought to defend his administration's cruel decision to separate migrant parents from their children at the U.S.-Mexico border, saying it prevented migrants from coming into the United States. Dozens of lawsuits have been filed against the federal government seeking damages for intentionally inflicting emotional distress on migrant families as a result of this practice.

Trump is likely to open the door to Putin and end NATO so that Putin could advance his need to build the USSR again. Trump will open the door to America, maybe politically, for Putin.

And in his bid for power, he quickly realized that appeals to identity could galvanize his political maga base. He had already, in the past, made a racist crusade of questioning Obama's birthplace. Now, he explicitly and enthusiastically embraced identity politics. He paints Black Americans with stereotypes as inherently poor and violent. He referred to Mexicans as criminal murderers and rapists. He spoke of Christian values despite numerous accusations of sexual assaults, while Judge Lewis Kaplan publicly said he was a rapist by legal definition. (Prem Thakker, New Republic, July 19, 2023.)

He has called women "horseface," "fat," and "ugly." Once sworn into office first term, he quickly instituted a travel ban on Muslims and called Haiti, El Salvador, and African nations "shithole" countries. He started building a "big, beautiful wall" along the border with Mexico, pulled out of international agreements, and started a trade war against China.

Trump retweeted a video of a retiree in Florida chanting "white power." He threatened to veto a defense spending bill to protect the legacy of *Confederate generals* on U.S. Army bases.

No Republican president in the past fifty years had ever pursued such an openly racist platform or championed white, evangelical Americans at the expense of everyone else. He is doing it today with more emphasis on immigration as an issue, planning per Project 2025, a second (or more) term with camps set up throughout the country to send the "illegals" to and then deport them, even if they were born in the US of immigrant parents, making them legal citizens by the constitution.

The plan has him reversing civil and voting rights laws with executive orders, proclamations, and specific administrative orders. These orders are published in the *Federal Register,* the daily journal of the federal government, to inform the public about federal regulations and actions. The National Archives then catalog them as official documents produced by the federal government. Both executive orders and proclamations have the complete force of law, much like regulations issued by federal agencies. They will be codified under Title 3 of the Code of Federal Regulations, which formally collects all the rules and regulations issued by the executive branch and other federal agencies.

Executive orders differ from legislation because they

don't need Congress's approval, and Congress cannot simply overturn them. Congress can pass laws that make enforcing the order difficult or even impossible, such as by cutting funding. Only a current U.S. President has the power to reverse an existing executive order by issuing a new one, which can take a significant amount of time in this situation.

The love and adoration that Trump's followers feel toward their Leader only grows the more dictatorial, fascistic, and hostile to human decency and traditional society he becomes. The *cruelty is always the point*; Trump hates the same people his followers do. Like other cult leaders, Trump's relationship with his MAGA followers is both parasitic and symbiotic.

Fascism, as a continuation of today's American conservatism, is a form of religious politics (a movement driven more by faith, action, and violence than by reason and reflection) that largely disregards empirical reality and the outdated everyday politics that the mainstream news media and larger political class blindly follow.

Overall, the MAGA movement and American neofascism are revolutionary efforts, built over decades, to dismantle multiracial pluralistic democracy and replace it with an American Christo-fascist Apartheid plutocracy. As seen with Project 2025, for example, the Republican fascists and "conservative" movement have made significant progress in developing the infrastructure to carry out these plans. (Professor Stanley, Yale University and author of "How Fascism Works").

There is a problem with a lack of national security. Each day, America has a president who feels the need to do something to draw attention to himself or to divert attention from the latest issue he may be facing with the public. Each day, he pays less attention to matters of global intelligence and issues important to the country's internal safety, while terrorist cells no doubt make plans both inside and outside the country.

Implementation and Incompetence

Many believe that government should be managed like a business, but this idea is far from the truth. Businesses and other organizations are best planned and operated using MBO, or "management by objectives," as developed by management guru Peter Drucker. A business is run to generate profit, entailing managing operations to earn more revenue than the costs incurred. In contrast, government is designed and established to serve the people who live in and depend on their country for its services and kindness—to help and to heal.

Medicaid, FEMA, Business loans, it is more than these.

The goal of the government is to fulfill America's promise at the base of Lady Liberty: "Give me your tired, your poor, your huddled masses yearning to breathe free, the wretched re-fuse of your teeming shore.

Send these, the homeless, tempest-tost to me, I lift my lamp be-side the golden door!" There are chains at the feet of the Statue of Liberty. The designer, Bartoli, saw these chains as a symbol of breaking free from the ongoing struggle and representing ra-cial equality, as outlined in our sacred documents.

History tells us the consequences of Autocracy, Fascism, and dictators.

Historians warn us about thinking like a "strongman." Citizens who want a "strongman" to "get things done" or to eliminate freedoms they dislike may find that once the "strongman" is elected, they've actually voted away their voting rights. The "strongman" no longer needs the support of those who believed he would be their protector. Instead of doing things like removing non-Christians and non-whites from the country, he won't prioritize citizens' wants or needs. His focus will be on his own interests, using taxes to address his legal and criminal issues.

The modern American fascist movement is fueled by oligarchical interests that see democracy as an obstacle to the public good, such as those in the energy and oil sectors. It also has social, political, and religious roots linked to the

Confederacy. Like all fascist movements, these forces have found a popular leader outside the bounds of democratic rules in Donald Trump.

The German Nazi Party significantly boosted its popularity over many years, partly by carefully hiding its explicit antisemitic agenda to attract moderate voters. These voters convinced themselves that the racism at the core of Nazi ideology was something the party had outgrown. The Nazis presented themselves as the solution to communism, pointing to a history of political violence—including street clashes between

communists and the far right—to warn of a potential violent communist takeover. They gained support from business leaders by promising to dismantle labor unions. The Nazis depicted socialists, Marxists, liberals, labor unions, the cultural sector, and the media as enemies or sympathizers of enemies. Once in power, they reinforced this message consistently.

We understand what happened when Fascism led to Hitler and Germany. Millions of Jews were brutally murdered, countries were invaded and occupied, and the slaughter of countless innocent civilians and soldiers in Europe and Russia should serve as a warning for American voters. We know what transpired when Mussolini became dictator; he used mustard gas on civilians and murdered the Red Cross in Ethiopia. The Italian army burned homes, razed villages, and destroyed farmland to strengthen his hold in Yugoslavia. (https://www.grunge.com/611314/how-mussolini-was-even-more-evil-than-you-think/)

When Stalin became dictator, millions were murdered and buried in unmarked graves. Putin, as a dictator, controls an oligarchy that siphons money from poor and suffering citizens while he and his henchmen amass fortunes so large they lose track of their total. The slightest threat to his power results in journalists being thrown from building windows, poisoned in their underwear, or dying in jail. Those he dislikes may find themselves in a sudden plane crash.

Trump has used his "us vs them" terminology to establish concentration camps, which ICE agents, masked and violent, are now filling, to round up nonwhite people, immigrant and citizen, then disappear them to foreign soil.

This is depleting the American labor force, helping to cripple the economy. Our fields, construction, domestic help, and hospitality industry are suffering under a need for labor.

Since Trump openly announced he would have his DOJ apprehend anyone who opposed him or his adversaries, he may have taken the cue from Putin to replenish his financial situation. He is exposed in court as a fraud and a consistent loser of his father's money. Being a dictator allows him to siphon tax and kick back dollars into his account. Putin has been doing this for many years. Trump is now running the most corrupt administration in history with absolute immunity.

Economics of democracy
MIT Study

A new study co-authored by an MIT economist shows when it comes to growth, democracy significantly increases economic development. Countries switching to democratic majority rule experience a 20 percent increase in GDP over 25 years, compared to what would have happened had they remained authoritarian states.

"I don't find it surprising that it should be a big effect because this is a big event and nondemocracies, dictatorships, are messed up in many dimensions," says Daron Acemoglu, an

MIT economist, and co-author of this new paper about the study. He notes that democracies employ broad-based investment, especially in health and human capital, which authoritarian states lack.

"Many growth-enhancing reforms eliminate special favors that nondemocratic regimes have done for their cronies. Democracies are much more pro-reform,"

The paper "Democracy Does Cause Growth" is published in the *Journal of Political Economy*. Acemoglu, Elizabeth, and James Killian, Professors of Economics at MIT are the authors.

Censorship of culture, reality, and history in GOP

Texas recently passed an unconstitutional law restricting what books can be assigned and subjects taught in the classroom. It barred teachers from discussing "controversial" current events and forced teachers to provide "opposing" perspectives on the Holocaust. In Iowa, teachers are to avoid telling their students about the Native American genocide by white men. (Powell, NYT June 22, 2021)

Wisconsin's anti-Critical Race Theory bill listed nearly ninety terms and concepts that would be forbidden if passed, including "unconscious bias," "equity," "hegemony," "multiculturalism," "white supremacy," and "racial justice."

(Henry Redman, Wisconsin Examiner, - January 26, 2022)

Florida, Missouri, and other states will soon allow private citizens to sue schools if kids are "taught, instructed, or compelled to express belief in, or support for" specific ideas about race, sex, or other matters or not offered courses giving "an overall positive . . . history and understanding of the United States." (Stanley, How Fascism Works, 2023)

So why not whitewash history? The subject of slavery and brutality is unsavory and may produce anxiety in young students.

"Our educational system often says little about slavery… " says Professor Muhammad of Harvard.

"It positions slavery, for example, as something that shouldn't have happened, but it wasn't that important because, well, we ended it, and so let's move on," he surmised. "But the truth is that what our students ought to be learning, that we can choose to teach them, is that there is no American history without Black people's contributions. There's no founding American wealth without the experience of enslaved Africans as the wealth generators for this nation." (Khalil Gibran Muhammad, Professor of History, Race & Policy, Harvard Kennedy School)

During this challenging time in our nation's history, as protests continue across the U.S. to fight against systemic injustice and violence toward Black people, Dr. Muhammad says it's now more important than ever to "get our history right."

Protest

Republican governors in several red states have signed legislation into law that makes protest a criminal act, despite the protections for protest granted by the Constitution, and even creates protections for drivers who run over demonstrators. More than forty of these bills have recently become law in twenty-three states, all enacted by Republicans, though four states—Florida, Arizona, Georgia, and Wisconsin—are not included. Many more have been introduced in other states by MAGA politicians. It is clear to a reader with even a basic understanding of the Constitution and its rules that none of these laws are constitutional. (Stanley, How Fascism Works, 2023)

These bills were passed in response to protest movements against police brutality, oil and gas pipelines, and college campus protests. Punishments may include hefty fines and jail time for blocking roads and sidewalks or being near pipelines, a broad definition of "rioting" that provides for loud talking which could cause protesters to be trapped, and making encouraging others to participate in an "unlawful assembly" punishable by jail. Many parts of these laws are unconstitutional, such as the First Amendment Right to

Assemble, which explicitly grants the right to protest. (Pepper, Saving Democracy, 2023)

The First Amendment protects the freedom to peaceful assembly, gathering, or association with a group of people for social, economic, political, or religious purposes. It also protects the right to protest the government. (Vidque.com Blog, 2023)

Writing a book is another form of free speech. Reading this book is another form of freedom of speech.

In this discussion about free speech, it is important to clarify the judicial use of "content neutrality" by courts. When deciding cases involving artistic freedom of expression, the Supreme Court relies on "content neutrality" for many of its free speech decisions. Content neutrality means that the government cannot censor or restrict expression simply because some part of the population finds the content offensive. (Freedom of Speech - Origins, First Amendment & Limits. https://www.history.com/topics/united-states-constitution/freedom-of-speech)

Challenges to the Republic in the 21st Century

The 45th President of the United States aimed to concentrate his power, ignoring the established norms that had protected American democracy for nearly two hundred fifty years. Under Trump, the nation experienced division, partly because many Republicans felt left behind and reacted against the changing civil liberties landscape. The ensuing culture wars, often trivial and absurd, fueled flames of violence and political dominance.

The Republican Party, once recognized for its diversity of thought, has taken a very different path. It has become a party that seeks to undermine American democracy. There is no simple way for the Republican Party to win elections or gain support for its issues, which mainly involve taking freedoms away from fellow citizens. Instead of welcoming a variety of voices and perspectives, it is determined to shape America into an exclusively white, autocratic stronghold.

First Amendment and the Christian-only GOP

"The Government of the United States of America is not, in any sense, founded on the Christian religion."

These words were placed in the 1796 Treaty of Tripoli by founding father and first vice-president John Adams; Washington never used religious words; Alexander Hamilton, in 1788, warned of the religious danger posed by an authoritarian leader at the helm of a democratic state, a scenario that echoes recent developments, Thomas Paine made no qualms about his radical Deism; calling the bible the "pretended word of God." And we know he's read it because he tears into it book by book in his writing *The Age of Reason*.

"Whenever we read the obscene stories, the voluptuous debaucheries, the cruel and tortuous executions, the unrelenting vindictiveness with which more than half the Bible is filled, it would be more consistent that we call it the word of a demon than the word of God,"

The First Amendment's Establishment Clause stops the government from merging with religious functions or officially endorsing religious doctrines. The Free Exercise Clause protects individuals' right to observe their religion without government coercion. These two clauses serve different purposes and prohibit two different kinds of government interference with religious freedom. The Free Exercise Clause relates to "governmental compulsion," while the Establishment Clause is violated by laws that establish an official religion, even if those laws do not directly force non-practicing individuals. The Free Exercise Clause defends individual religious beliefs, whereas the Establishment Clause addresses institutional efforts to promote political power or undermine civil authority. (history.com 2003, Freedom of Speech)

How did that guy get elected?

The newfound success of political bullying was not acceptable in American political history before 2016 and Trump, as far as I know. Bullying had not been widely used in campaigns before, but it seemed to work for him. He did not need to understand policy, economics, or politics. He did not need to be intelligent or kind. As it turned out, the other candidates were limp flowers, intimidated by the playground-style names he gave them, and soon found themselves alone among the other contenders.

Donald Trump's presidential campaigns were characterized by a distinctive communication style that some have described as "bullying." Here are a few ways this may have helped him win:

Labeling opponents: Trump uses unflattering nicknames for his competitors, such as "Lyin' Ted," which may have influenced voters' perceptions of these candidates. In past elections of such a high level, the voters may have thought such a tactic awkward and silly.

Aggressive rhetoric: Trump's speeches and tweets often contained controversial statements. This confrontational style drew significant media attention, increasing his visibility—the more shocking, the more coverage he received. For example: Mexican immigrants are murderers and rapists, coming across our southern border, a remark he made when riding the escalator down at his announcement for candidacy.

Appeal to sure voters: Some voters may have been drawn to Trump's assertive style, viewing it as a sign of strength and a break from traditional political discourse.

Psychological repositioning: By attacking his opponents, Trump may have psychologically repositioned them in the eyes of voters. (How Marketing Helped Elect Donald Trump, Washington Post 2017)

I only need to comment on Trump's use of "little" Marco Rubio, who is now a lapdog in Trump's cabinet. Trump knocked Jeb Bush out of the race when he complained that Bush was not wearing a suit to campaign. Trump would never be seen outside of a suit, as it covers his obesity — at least, that is my thought. The only pictures of him seemingly out of public sight are on the golf course, where he appears in all his obese glory.

He called the FBI director "Slippery" James Comey, who he is now "going after" through his DOJ. He put the security of the U.S. in nuclear danger by calling Kim Jong-un of North Korea "Little Rocket Man." Elizabeth Warren became Pocahontas.

Under normal circumstances, such clownish behavior would have ended his political career. But it turns out that childish conduct is actually part of his "charisma."

When nominated, it was arrogant to tell his audience that "I alone can fix" all the problems he and his party created that America was expected to suffer from.

His bullying seems to be making cowards of our justice

system. Any other citizen would be in jail for the comments and bullying he directs at the media and social media despite a gag order.

Trump's Silver Spoon

President number 45-47 of the United States received 413 million dollars USD tax-free illegally, as reported in the New York Times several years ago. The Times reported that President Donald Trump received at least $413 million from his father over the decades, much of that through dubious tax dodges, including outright fraud. (October 2, 2018, New York Times (A.P.)

With that money, he tried to be a successful money

maker yet declared bankruptcy at least six times, leaving many real estate projects and business ventures in his wake. With that money, he faked management prowess in his own "Trump Organization," being the fellow who could hire and fire at will.

His accountant kept the management of the place in somewhat capable yet corrupt hands, which the State of New York charged his organization and later him with, and found him guilty of fraud. At the same time, Trump took credit for all the constant PR, consisting of little more than bravado, smoke, and mirrors, making it seem like he made big money wherever he went.

He played his role for years on TV, and many less knowledgeable viewers believed his behavior reflected what management was all about: the rigid, mean, lying, unyielding mafia type who would run over anyone in his way. That was the part he played in his television "reality" show, and it was the act he benefited from. He maintained this persona during his campaign for President and continued to play the same role as President. He fired most of the people he initially hired as President. Those skilled individuals who knew more than he did were the first to be dismissed — in the past, Presidents usually hired people who were more intelligent and talented. Trump hired unconditional love dogs wherever he could find them.

He attracted voters who believed problems could be solved through violence, seemingly intimidated by the educated and sophisticated classes. During rallies for Trump's campaign, he told his audience to punch protesters in the face, and some did. The bullying class respects bullying; diplomacy and civility are not understood and are seen as signs of weakness, not respected, and no one knows how to practice them. Often, these are men and women raised to respect violent behavior and who have had no chance to learn any other way.

The bullying and calls to violence revealed the people left behind by the educated and the civilized, who always seemed to be elected President. Before 45, voters wanted their President to be considerate, intelligent, sophisticated, educated, and honest. Or so many voters believed. These were the very people these left-behind voters did not understand. These upper-class politicians did not experience the frustration of being disrespected or what it means to be unable to earn an "elite" amount of money. The candidate who could not explain away lies, dishonesty, or who had questionable morals was not nominated or elected before bullying and lies changed the political landscape.

Where did these trump people come from?

And why do they now want a dictator over a democracy? One theory is that:

The 2008 financial crisis and the 2010 deregulation of campaign contributions in the United States increased the influence of the wealthy and diminished that of voters. As economic inequality grew, people's time horizons shortened, and fewer Americans believed that the future would be a better version of the present. Without a functional state that provides basic social goods—such as education, pensions, health care, transportation, parental leave, and vacations—that are taken for granted elsewhere, Americans could become overwhelmed by everyday life and lose hope for the future.

Authoritarianism gone amuck

What most defines Donald Trump supporters? They're white? They're poor? They're uneducated?

In fact, research has shown that a single statistically significant variable predicts whether a voter supports Trump — and it's not race, income, or education levels: it's authoritarianism, although college and graduate degrees are much more anti-authoritarian.

Trump's electoral strength and durability mainly stem from Americans with authoritarian tendencies. Because of the widespread presence of authoritarians among the American electorate, including both Democrats and Republicans, Trump's supporter base could continue to grow.

This finding is based on a nationwide poll conducted in the last five days of December under the auspices of the

University of Massachusetts, Amherst. The poll surveyed 1,800 registered voters across the political spectrum. A standard statistical analysis showed that education, income, gender, age, ideology, and religiosity did not significantly influence a Republican voter's preferred candidate. Only two variables were statistically significant: authoritarianism and fear of terrorism.

Authoritarianism is not a new or untested idea among the American people. Since the rise of Nazi Germany, the concept has been one of the most thoroughly studied in social science. While its causes remain debated, the political behavior of authoritarians is clear. Authoritarians obey, rally behind, and follow strong leaders. They also react aggressively to outsiders, especially when they feel threatened. From pledging to "make America great again" by building a wall on the border to promising to close mosques and ban Muslims from visiting the United States, Trump is appealing directly to authoritarian tendencies.

Not all authoritarians are Republicans. Since 1992, many have identified as independents and Democrats in national surveys. In the 2008 Democratic primary, political scientist Marc Hetherington found that authoritarianism was a stronger predictor of voter preference for Hillary Clinton over Barack Obama than income, ideology, gender, age, or education. However, Hetherington has also observed, based on 14 years of polling, that authoritarians have consistently shifted from the Democratic to the Republican Party over time. He hypothesizes that this trend started decades ago as Democrats began to embrace civil rights, gay rights, employment protections, and other positions emphasizing freedom and equality. According to the poll results mentioned, authoritarianism has not been a statistically significant factor in the Democratic primary so far. Still, it appears to play a crucial role on the Republican side. In fact, 49 percent of likely Republican primary voters surveyed scored in the top quarter of the authoritarian scale—more than twice as many as Democratic voters.

Political pollsters have overlooked a crucial aspect of Trump's support because they do not include questions about authoritarianism in their surveys. In addition to the usual demographic, horse race, thermometer-scale, and policy questions, the poll also asked four simple survey questions that political scientists have used since 1992 to measure authoritarian tendencies. These questions focus on child-rearing: whether it is more important for a voter to want a child who is respectful or independent, obedient or self-reliant, well-behaved or considerate, and well-mannered or curious. Respondents who pick the first option in each question are strongly authoritarian.

Based on these questions, Trump was the only candidate—Republican or Democrat—whose support among authoritarians was statistically significant.

So, what does this mean for the Trump phenomenon? It not only helps us understand what motivates Trump's supporters, but also indicates that his backing isn't limited. In a statistical analysis of polling results, Trump has already secured 43 percent of Republican primary voters who are strong authoritarians, and 37 percent of Republican authoritarians overall. A majority of Republican authoritarians in my poll also strongly supported Trump's proposals to deport 11 million illegal immigrants, ban Muslims from entering the United States, shut down mosques, and establish a nationwide database to track Muslims.

And Trump's strongman rhetoric appeals to some of the 39 percent of independents who identify as authoritarians and the 17 percent of self-identified Democrats who are strong authoritarians.

Furthermore, the number of Americans worried about the threat of terrorism is increasing. In 2011, Hetherington published research showing that non-authoritarians respond to perceived threats by acting more like authoritarians. As fear and threats grow, more voters are vulnerable to Trump's message about protecting Americans. 52 percent of those who are most afraid that another terrorist attack will happen in the next 12 months are non-authoritarians—prime targets for Trump's message.

So, those who claimed a Trump presidency "can't happen here" should reconsider their assumptions. The candidate has defied traditional expectations because those expectations are based on an oversimplified view of the electorate in general and his supporters specifically. The conditions are perfect for an authoritarian leader, and now it's happening. Trump is exploiting this situation. Meanwhile, institutions—from the Republican Party to the press—that are supposed to prevent what James Madison called "the infection of violent passions" among the people have either been intimidated by Trump's bravado or are neglecting their responsibilities.

It's time for those who would appeal to our better angels to take his insurgency seriously and stop dismissing his supporters as a small band of the dispossessed. Trump support is firmly rooted in American authoritarianism and, now fully awakened, it is a force to be reckoned with.

Matthew MacWilliams is founder of MacWilliams Sanders, a political communications firms, and a Ph.D. in political science from the University of Massachusetts, Amherst, where his dissertation is about authoritarianism.

Understanding the 1/6 Insurrection Through Terror Management Theory

Terror Management Theory provides a unique perspective on the motivations behind the January 6th insurrection at the U.S. Capitol. This theory, which explores how the fear of death shapes human behavior and beliefs, can shed light on the participants' seemingly irrational support and actions during this unprecedented event. (Phillips, Ivory. "Battling for the Development and Survival of Genuine American Democracy." Jackson Advocate, vol. 83, no. 41, 2021, p. 4B.)

Certain age groups may appear most vulnerable. I noticed many retired-age individuals in the insurrection video. It's not a scientific study, just a personal observation. They also seemed to display characteristics of the left-behind class.

The 1/6 insurrection can be examined through the TMT lens:

1.   Worldview Defense:

The insurrectionists, many of whom were strong supporters of President Trump, saw their political and cultural beliefs as under threat after the 2020 presidential election results. TMT suggests that in such situations, people tend to react defensively to defend their views, such as their belief in

Trump's leadership and the claims of a "stolen" election.

2.   Mortality as Reality:

Leading up to the insurrection, there was a rise in rhetoric about losing traditional values and the perceived end of a certain way of life. This rhetoric probably increased mortality salience among supporters, prompting them to rally strongly in defense of their beliefs.

3.   Group Identity and Self-esteem:

TMT also indicates that self-esteem relates to cultural values and group identity. By acting in ways they believed protected their group's values, the insurrectionists may have attempted to boost their self-esteem and sense of importance, especially amid feelings of marginalization.

4.   Reaction to Threat:

According to TMT, when individuals perceive their worldview as under threat, they may resort to extreme measures to defend it. The violent and unlawful actions on January 6th could be interpreted as an expression of this existential anxiety and an attempt to preserve their perceived way of life.

Terror Management Theory offers a framework for understanding events like the January 6th insurrection. By analyzing the actions of participants through the lens of existential fear and the need to defend their worldviews, we can better understand the motivations behind what might otherwise seem like irrational support and behaviors. This perspective helps us comprehend such events and emphasizes the importance of addressing existential fears and beliefs.

The truth does not matter.

Liz Cheney – "Growing up in a political family, you often learn early that some people who act like friends are actually opportunists — sometimes wealthy individuals seeking to get close to those in office. This woman and her husband turned out to be people I had completely misjudged. She and my mother had gone to Wyoming Girls State together in the 1950s. I believed I could trust her, that she had the integrity to listen and understand what was happening. I told her how the courts had ruled. I gave Her the facts—what Bill Barr was saying, what the Constitution required. When Dallin Oaks, president of the Mormon Church, to which she belonged, made remarks about our duty to the Constitution, I sent them to her. President Oaks' remarkable statement included the lines: "We are to be governed by law and not by individuals, and our loyalty is to the Constitution and its principles and processes, not to any office holder.

But nothing could break the spell that QAnon had cast over her. She threw away a friendship of over 60 years with my mother and my family for nothing. I also found that many of those in Wyoming who were the most upset or angry were unaware of the violence on January 6. They believed the day to have been almost entirely peaceful. They read The Epoch Times, a "news" website that presents extremely slanted reporting in the guise of a straightforward media outlet. They believed what they saw on their social media feeds. They watched Fox News, Newsmax, and OAN almost exclusively. As a result, they were completely unaware of what had actually happened. More than a few believed that I should be pressing for Joe Biden's removal from office and Donald Trump's reinstallation as president." (Liz cheney, Oath and Honor)

How Lies Become Facts

Some people grow up in families where gossip serves as a form of entertainment, isolated from other perspectives and realities by the level of education, intelligence, income, and choice of living space. Direct communication may be with neighbors with the same class, education, and lifestyle. Stories and gossip, "Trump supporters are attempting to circumvent the Constitution." may be made up or interpreted as truth, then passed on to others as the gospel. The more bizarre the made-up truth is, the more entertaining it may be; thus, it is more in demand. They may also live in neighborhoods where a dominant source of information, such as Fox "news," spreads opinions and lies as facts. And that is the source of lies as facts.

Some organizations also spread falsehoods as facts, including paramilitary groups and white supremacists who support the QAnon movement. The QAnon phenomenon often involves conspiracy theories, such as the claim that a secret cabal of satanic pedophiles and cannibals controls the world and plots against former President Trump. Because of this connection, the Trump cult has direct ties to QAnon and white power groups. Some people believe these falsehoods without questioning their sources or evidence. The group becomes an echo chamber, and the person sharing the false information is seen as a trusted friend who always tells the truth as part of the tribe, even if it's a lie.

And what juicy lies they are. The concerning part is that those who accept lies as truth don't care if there is accurate empirical evidence supporting the stories. There is no concern for truth or lies as separate entities, as described in Terror Management Theory.

The context in which a lie is told matters. Some people may not be able to tell the difference between news and entertainment or opinion. Many trust whatever they hear on their preferred media, even if it's biased or false. Too many lack the education or critical thinking skills to judge the credibility and truth of the information they receive.

Education can teach people the importance of evidence and proof in supporting statements. It can make people critical and skeptical of the information they encounter, wherever it comes from. Without education, lies can become the truth for some people.

Journalism classes stress the importance of objectivity, accuracy, and fairness in news reporting. Journalists are expected to cite reliable sources and provide evidence for their claims. However, some media outlets have abandoned these principles and resorted to sensationalism, propaganda, and misinformation, presenting opinions and lies as news and using other opinions as evidence. There is a tendency to appeal to the emotions and prejudices of the audience rather than reason and logic.

What would happen if all media were required to have sources and solid evidence to back up their news reports? Why does Fox News employ people skilled at fabricating entertaining political lies as if they are legitimate reporters? Too many media outlets present opinions as facts, based on other opinions as evidence. Even worse, news is often based on what a political leader claims as truth. This damages the public and democracy. I had an uneducated parent who gossiped with neighbors as a way of life. Most of the gossip was made up, unsubstantiated, and further exaggerated with entertainment when passed on to others. Everyone in my family knew Mother was a drama queen who thrived on false narratives, and that was just who she was.

As kids, we went to school learning about science and connecting a theory or hypothesis through experimentation to gather proof from the testing results. My mother had no such knowledge. She came from parents, one who had never been to school, and the other who dropped out at eighth grade to work, who did not understand this comparison of talk and theory to solid evidence and correlations.

For years, media reported news through reliably educated journalists like Walter Cronkite, who wouldn't publish a story until it was verified. Then came cable TV and newer media, whose leaders discovered a large audience that thrives on drama and stories lacking facts, with no regard for the difference between the two as long as it fueled their emotional beliefs.

Since cable TV became popular, fact-based network news has declined due to profit motives. The audience for this type of news often lacks critical thinking skills, similar to high school students who simply attend class or participate in sports and get a passing grade. There's not always a need to work hard or understand the connection between hypothesis, evidence, and truth. Gossip is often much more entertaining. Therefore, with cable TV, the news media focus on personalities, gossip, and occasionally politics. This approach is profitable for large right-wing media outlets, where political gossip is common and integrity or proof are not necessary. Massive profits are generated through advertising products like gold, cars, and other items that sell well among those who do not read but watch and absorb conspiracy theories and wild stories about left-leaning politicians.

Let's take it a step further. Sociolinguists recognize that when the collection of words, stories, or concepts becomes too dominant in our thoughts, it shapes our reality, leading us to hear things that aren't actually said and see things that align with our beliefs but are not real events.

Now we have leaders who want to stay aligned with bullying political opponents, who will take any story and believe it without evidence, testing, or verified facts as long as it supports their stance. If the leader tells us to drink bleach, it might become a perceived reality, and their supporters believe it as if it's proven, even if the "tested evidence" is just another story. Our leader claims that bleach will cure us and help us survive a life-threatening disease. Are we surprised when parts of our population end up in hospitals and emergency rooms for poisoning? Lies breed more lies, creating false evidence to support the original falsehoods as truth. Call it a world of words gone off the rails and dangerous.

MAGA members live in a world where only the ideas they want to be real are real, as explained by Terror Management Theory. There is no solid science linking the world of falsehoods to the real world. They don't need to see Santa climbing down a chimney or eating the cookies left out for him; they have an unwavering belief in Santa Claus. Trump told MAGA voters early on that real-world media is fake, and they want it that way and are sticking to it.

Facts are wars, societal breakdowns, mass shootings, incivility on airplanes and elsewhere, the Supreme Court, jobs, the economy, freedom of choice, dictators, and MAGA. Facts are based on solid evidence — see it, touch it, feel it — never on the spinning of stories or conspiracy theories.

Authoritarianism concerns anyone whose practices are disapproved of—exactly what the founding fathers aimed to overcome—especially when it involves racism, giving racism a platform, and related issues like immigration, immigrants, and border politics.

Believe in truth.

To abandon facts is to abandon freedom. If nothing is true, then no one can criticize power because there is no basis for doing so. If nothing is true, then all is spectacle. The biggest wallet pays for the most blinding lights. (From: On Tyranny, T Snyder)

America is on a Road to Fascism

Fascist politicians distort history to create a narrative that fits their current agenda. These politicians use language manipulation and propaganda to alter public perception, often targeting educational institutions that oppose their views. This strategy encourages a climate where conspiracy theories and misinformation replace rational discussion, leading to a state of "unreality" where harmful and false beliefs spread. (from "Why Evolution Is True" October 8, 2022)

A The core belief of fascist ideology is to promote the idea of inherent group differences, falsely justifying a hierarchy of human worth. This mindset divides society and fosters fear and hostility among different groups. Progress by minority communities is seen as a threat to the majority, creating a sense of victimhood. You might hear things like, "If they were not so lazy and stupid, they could have what any American has." Politicians who exploit this trend often divide society into "us," the law-abiding citizens, and "them," the lawless elements threatening national identity. These are the "vermin." As a result, you get the racist narrative of "immigrants" as Mexicans crossing the border, labeled as "murderers and rapists." This division conveniently acts as a subtle racial signal.

Furthermore, fascist politics is often associated with anxiety when traditional gender roles are challenged, such as the belief that there are only two sexes. Amid these changes, those who hold to "traditional" values are portrayed as virtuous, living in rural areas as strongholds of national values and traditions, untouched by urban diversity, reminiscent of 1950. Conversely, "others" are depicted as exploiters of welfare systems and corrupters of institutions like labor unions meant to protect the interests of the hardworking working class.

The complex ideological structure of Fascism and its connected elements are not always clear. The political slogans, like "America first," which has roots in the Ku Klux Klan, are part of a larger strategy to manipulate and shape public perception.

Putin's fascism

Former Russian Foreign Minister Andrei Kozyrev recently commented that Putin sees in Trump.

"A leader who would undermine American democracy and diminish its role as a stabilizing force capable of containing Putin."

Trump's appearance on Russian Television (RT) and his criticisms of the media align with Putin's style of influence. This connection suggests that Trump has been following a strategy similar to Putin's, possibly under his guidance, becoming a tool for Russian interests. Through Russian media outlets like Sputnik, Trump has been seen as someone who helps weaken Western influence and shifts history to favor Russia's geopolitical goals.

A Russian oligarch, Dmitry Rybolovlev, purchased a property from Trump for $55 million more than Trump had paid, showed no interest in it, and never resided there. Later, when Trump ran for president, Rybolovlev frequently appeared at Trump's campaign events. Trump's seemingly business venture, real estate development, appeared to be a Russian charade for money laundering. (The Road to Unfreedom, Snyder, 2023)

Having realized that apartment complexes could be used to launder money, Russians used Trump's name to build more buildings. As Donald Trump Jr. said in 2008, "We see a lot of money pouring in from Russia." (Friedman, NYT, February 18, 2018)

The Friedman article in the New York Times goes on to say:

"President Trump is either compromised by the Russians or is a towering fool, or both, but either way, he has shown himself unwilling or unable to defend America against a Russian campaign to divide and undermine our democracy."

While much of Friedman's column was speculation, the decade-old quote from Trump Jr. of 2008 sheds light on the Trump family's past financial holdings, though it does not implicate the Trumps in any illegal activity.

Liberals have used Trump Jr.'s words to illustrate their belief that Russia may have leverage over Trump because of his previous business dealings in the country.

"My guess is what Trump is hiding has to do with money," Friedman said. "It's something about his financial ties to business elites tied to the Kremlin. They may own a big stake in him." (Friedman, NYT, February 18, 2018)

Given Trump's reliance on Russia to maintain his appearance of success and survival, is there any doubt about what was happening between Trump and Putin during those calls and meetings where he destroyed records of their conversations? It is also noticeable that any criticism or questioning of Putin, when asked about Trump, only results in praise. Is there any doubt now that becoming a powerful dictator of America is beyond Trump, or is he just trying to avoid jail?

Trump is taking steps toward becoming a dictatorial leader, such as attacking institutions, undermining the rule of law, and similar actions. Trump will deny losing in 2024, and then the MAGA House will declare him the winner through state legislatures, using the MAGA phrase, "We are a "constitutional republic," not a 'democracy,'" even though elections don't work for us. So, here is the MAGA party trying to dismantle the current system of government and replace it with a dictator like Trump, following the Project 2025 plan to eliminate all enemies and deal with them. Of course, Trump, who has been losing money since his father gave him over $400 million in illegal gifts, will adopt a playbook similar to Putin's. As a dictator, he will drain taxpayer money and amass real wealth, becoming truly, truly rich.

Meanwhile, the Democrats are coasting along on their political scooters, talking about how crucial the next election is, even if the opposition ignores it to put their boy Trump into office regardless, and much time and effort are spent on those Democrat elections rather than addressing and preventing the end of democracy.

Lies, A Hammer To The Head, Putin Politics

The Russian philosopher Ivan Ilyin was a key figure whose ideas heavily shaped Russian politics, especially during Putin's presidency. His philosophy is used to justify and plan actions such as undermining the European Union and invading

Ukraine. Ilyin supported authoritarian rule, violence, and the use of propaganda and lies. Putin highlighted Ilyin's ideas in his speeches after the fall of the USSR. Putin marched into Crimea and occupied it with "fake" news. He fed the press the idea that Russia was being put upon by having its rightful land ripped from its cold, dead hands. His thesis: If Europe and the United

States had done the right thing, Russia would have never lost what it had as a supreme power. And without even visiting that country, Rand Paul, the man against any war, was suddenly backing Putin and his war. Putin sees history and the history of Russia not in a historical context of progress but as a constant flux of the same things happening repeatedly, and the way things have been in the grand days is how it should be now. (Snyder, The Road To Unfreedom, 2019)

The way Russia was, the mighty USSR, is what

"should" occur, and the world should help it, per Putin. Putin used the Russian philosopher's variation of disinformation to the globe to include Europe, Russia, and the U.S. While attacking Ukraine. Putin's take on what was happening became the focus of media interpretation rather than media checking on the facts in the world. The press found it less of a hassle to hear what Putin said and what people who bought into Putin's lies said. And who says what has become the easy facts to gather and report on worldwide? Just reporting politicians' take on the situation seems to be the new norm. Trump picked up on that.

In front of a VFW club in 2018, Trump, as President of the U.S., said, *"Stick with us. Don't believe the crap you see from these people, the fake news. … What you're seeing and what you're reading is not what's happening." (July 24, 2018, Donald Trump to the VFW convention in Kansas City.)*

The message is to listen and believe him, or, as it turned out, only see and read what media he wants you to see, such as Fox, Newsmax, and other right-wing networks—this is a tactic from Putin's playbook. The work of disinformation and lies may have successfully done its job. Not only did his audience realize it then, but they continue to this day, aware that his disinformation is full of lies, yet they do not care, as they want to see the toxic issues of the GOP come to fruition. (Lavitsky, Tyranny Of The Minority, 2023)

Trump's Supreme Court gained influence after Mitch McConnell's unconstitutional move to delay Obama's Supreme Court nominee for a full year before the next elections, allowing a Republican president to appoint highly conservative justices. The divisive issue America feared surfaced as the new MAGA SCOTUS overturned Roe v. Wade, making abortion illegal again, much to the dismay of nearly 90% of the American voting public. Gun control laws, supported by over 90%, have not been enacted due to a minority in power, despite nearly daily mass shootings with assault weapons. Sexual freedom, as interpreted in the Civil Rights Act, is being rolled back, and racism and discrimination—from voting rights to America's history of slavery—are being modified where possible.

Civil Rights

Our Declaration of Independence sets the tone for The

Civil Rights Act of 1964, ending segregation in public places

and prohibiting discrimination based on race, ethnicity, religion, sex, or national origin.

"We hold these truths to be self-evident, that *all men are created equal, that their Creator endows them with certain unalienable Rights*, that among these are Life, Liberty and the pursuit of Happiness." (The thirteen United States of America, July 4, 1776)

Before the Act of 1964, African Americans, in particular, faced significant challenges due to discrimination that was legally sanctioned at the time. These included discrimination in employment, limited access to quality housing, disenfranchisement, and ongoing struggles to integrate public schools even ten years after Brown v. Board of Education of Topeka. The most important achievement of the civil rights movement in the 1950s and 60s was the Civil Rights Act, which expanded social and economic opportunities for African Americans and other minorities nationwide. The EEOC, or Equal Employment Opportunity Commission, was created to oversee employment discrimination. It prohibited racial discrimination and increased access to resources for women, religious minorities, African Americans, and low-income families. Furthermore, the Civil Rights Act of 1964 set the stage for subsequent civil rights laws, such as the Voting Rights Act of 1965 for African Americans and other minority groups, including the elimination of barriers to voting, protections against discrimination in renting, buying, or paying for housing (Fair Housing Act of 1968), and legal protections for Americans with disabilities (Americans with Disabilities Act of 1990).

In today's political landscape, a segment within the GOP, known for its extremist views, seeks to undermine civil rights, ignore the Constitution, and return to a time when minority freedoms were heavily restricted. This includes efforts to suppress minority voting in red states through tactics such as voter ID laws, gerrymandering, limited access to polling locations, reduced voting hours, and voter intimidation. College campuses, viewed as hubs of potential opposition, are also targeted to restrict voting.

The GOP has realized that their policies, like abortion bans and social security cuts, are very unpopular. To counter this, they have been undermining democratic norms, stacking the courts with conservative judges, and making it harder for nonwhite and other groups to vote.

The Electoral College, which allows presidential candidates who lose the popular vote to still win the election, makes the democratic process more complicated. The GOP aims to reshape the system to fit their agenda, creating what some call the "new confederacy."

While Democrats focus on winning at the federal level, the GOP concentrates on local elections to enact and solidify their policies. They spread the "Big Lie" that Trump won the 2020 election; thus, MAGA questioned the outcome of the 2024 election unnecessarily. The GOP's strategy relies on undermining democracy at the local level, replacing officials who upheld election integrity, and ensuring their political desires become a permanent reality.

MAGA supporters and 47 are attempting to circumvent the Constitution.

Suppression of Protest and Dissent

Many states have passed laws that criminalize protests and protect drivers who harm demonstrators. These laws were created in response to protests against issues like police brutality and pipeline projects. They impose hefty fines and jail time for blocking roads, even during peaceful demonstrations.

These laws raise serious constitutional concerns. The First Amendment protects the right to peaceful assembly, gather people for various purposes, and the freedom to protest the government. Despite these legal protections, these recently enacted laws infringe on fundamental rights. Recently, Trump began issuing orders to send troops wherever protests may occur, hoping to incite violence so he can declare an emergency and deploy even more troops to more blue cities and states, to use this emergency as a reason to avoid holding elections. Especially mid-term elections.

Local elections and legislatures

Maga Republicans are leveraging local elections to push harmful policies by taking advantage of the low turnout and the lack of attention that local races often get. They also use their influence and resources to back candidates who share their extreme views and agenda, while opposing those who challenge them. Some examples of the unpopular policies that Maga has enacted include:

Laws that ban or restrict abortion access, such as requiring waiting periods, mandatory ultrasounds, parental consent, and gestational limits, jeopardize the health and lives of women seeking reproductive care. (Abbott, Law and politics, Business Insider, 2021-06-13)

Laws that oppose public health measures, such as banning mask mandates, vaccine passports, and lockdowns, ignore scientific evidence and expert advice, risking the lives of millions of Americans from COVID-19 and its variants.

There are now laws that promote discrimination and bigotry, such as allowing businesses to refuse service to LGBTQ+ people, banning transgender athletes from participating in sports, and prohibiting the teaching of critical race theory in schools. All of these are part of the MAGA effort to remove these freedoms. These laws violate the civil rights and dignity of marginalized groups, creating a climate of hate and intolerance. (Penumaka, Republicans' Actions and Policies Are Toxically Unpopular, August 5, 2021)

MAGA Republicans are using local elections to push unpopular policies because they know they can't win on the national stage with their radical and divisive agenda. They attempt to impose their will on most Americans who don't share their vision for the country, and that's why voters need to pay attention to local elections and vote for candidates who represent their values and interests.

It is also true of a Senate that greatly underrepresents larger states and a gerrymandered House of Representatives. The system favors the old over the young, whites over nonwhites, and declining rural areas over growing metropolitan regions.

Supreme Court decisions also weakened the protections of the Voting Rights Act and increased the influence of concentrated money in politics, worsening these issues.

The Electoral College.

Over the 172 years from the widespread adoption of popular voting for President in 1824 until 1996, there were 44 elections. In only three of these, the winner of the popular vote differed from the Electoral College winner. Even in 1824, the popular vote winner, Andrew Jackson, secured a plurality in the Electoral College. However, since he lacked a majority, the election was decided by the House of Representatives, which chose the second-place finisher, John Quincy Adams. Partly due to outrage over this result, Jackson decisively defeated Adams four years later. In 1876, the election results from three southern states were highly contested, making it difficult to determine the exact popular vote. Only in 1888, when President Grover Cleveland lost reelection despite winning the popular vote by 0.8 percent, did a clear case of an Electoral College/popular vote split occur during this period. (General Andrew Jackson of the American Army. https://www.mywarof1812.com/leaders/jackson-andrew/)

However, two of the five elections between 2000 and 2016 involved a disparity between the popular and the electoral vote.

Over the past 50 years, a significant demographic shift has occurred, with an increasing number of people moving from rural areas to larger metropolitan regions, allowing the minority in our political system to dominate the majority.

In the Electoral College, every state, even California, which has a population of 42 million, automatically gets two electors—one for each of its two U.S. Senators—while Nebraska, with a population of 1.5 million, also receives two. Again, regardless of size, every state is allotted at least one elector for its member in Congress. Smaller states, which tend to be more rural, therefore have a significant advantage over larger, more populated states. Candidates favored by urban voters can secure large margins in cities and suburbs, but these wins are not always reflected in their electoral vote totals.

California has 67 times more people than Wyoming. (In the first Census, the ratio between the largest and smallest states was only 13-to-1.) California gets one elector for every 713,637 people, and Wyoming one for every 195,167. Therefore, in practical terms, a Wyoming voter has more than three and a half times the electoral power of a California voter. ("Is Democracy a 'fetish?'" The Hutchinson News, vol., no., 2016, p. 15)

In the case of the 2016 election, the Electoral College's distance from the popular vote was aggravated because so many Clinton voters cast ballots in large, reliably Democratic states like California and New York. Her big margins in these states had no payoff in the electoral vote.

Yet, it is only one part of our system that increasingly promotes minority rule. Look at the makeup of the Senate, where the small-state advantage is even more obvious than in the Electoral College. The 2016 election resulted in a Senate with 52 Republicans and 48 Democrats, including two Independents who caucus with the Democrats. Since highly populated states tend to vote Democratic, the 48 Democrats represent 55 percent of the nation's population. This also shows the bias created by the Senate's representation system, which favors rural interests over those of urban and metropolitan areas. For example, on gun control votes, the senators who oppose firearm regulations often represent a majority of the people, as clear from polls showing broad support for reforms like background checks. Budget decisions also reflect this bias: farm subsidies are much harder to cut than urban revitalization programs.

In April 2017, The Washington Post's Philip Bump published an article underscoring how unrepresentative the Senate has become. He noted,

A bill or nomination could pass out of the Senate with support from only 16.2 percent of the population. If the two senators from the 25 smallest states agreed to support a bill—and Vice President Pence concurred—the senators from the other 25 states and 270 million people they represent would be out of luck.

When Neil Gorsuch was confirmed to a lifetime appointment on the Supreme Court after a contentious battle, Bump noted that the senators voting for him represented only 44.4 percent of the population. In appointing the then-49-year-old, highly conservative Gorsuch to the Court, senators representing a minority of Americans made a decision that could shape the course of American law for decades.

By 2040, 70 percent of Americans will live in the 15 largest states. "That means that 70 percent of Americans get all 30 Senators, and 30 percent get 70 Senators. "(Wisnieski of City Limits. D\u27Anieri, Thomas. " David Birdsell, a political science professor at Baruch College, predicts (Healthy and *Unhealthy Responses to American Democratic Institutional Failure."* 2020.) *(https://core.ac.uk/pdf.)*

The House of Representatives

Theoretically, as its name suggests, the most representative government branch has become much less so because of partisan gerrymandering. Gerrymandering is an old American story. In its basic form, the majority party in a state legislature, seeking to maximize its representation, packs supporters of the minority party into a few districts where the opposition almost always wins by large margins—the minority party's supporters "waste" their votes in these landslide elections. The mapmakers then draw districts to create an even more secure majority by making their candidates win by comfortable but smaller margins.

Both parties have engaged in gerrymandering, but because of the Republicans' 2010 sweep, they controlled the most recent redistricting process in nearly all key swing states. Republicans already hold an advantage over Democrats in the House due to the concentration of Democratic votes in urban areas. Aggressive Republican gerrymandering has amplified this bias. David Wasserman of The Cook Political Report calculated that Democrats won 50.5 percent of all major-party votes in House elections in 2012 but only 46.2 percent of the seats. In 2014, Democrats received 47.1 percent of the vote but only 43.2 percent of the seats.

The Electoral College, gerrymandering, and making it hard to vote gave Maga much more power than the Constitution and founders saw coming. These local legislatures and school boards need to be cleaned of the maga influence and replaced with people true to Democracy.

Ending gerrymandering wouldn't be a fix-all for our political system. However, removing it would definitely lead to fairer and stronger competition. In May 2017, the Brennan Center for Justice responded to those who dismiss the effect of partisan redistricting. The center's Extreme Maps report showed that in 26 states, which make up 85 percent of congressional districts, Republicans gain a net advantage of at least 16 seats because of partisan bias in districting. When the report was published, Democrats only needed to flip 24 seats to take the House majority—meaning that about two-thirds of the GOP's advantage could be due to gerrymandering. (Extreme Maps | Brennan Center for Justice. https://www.brennancenter.org/our-work/research-reports/extreme-maps?)

Democrats have realized they must focus on winning state legislative seats. Less-partisan districting can be achieved if parties split control of state legislatures or if one party can counter the other's legislative majorities by winning governorships.

The gerrymandering issue is crucial for Congress and state legislatures. The distorted district boundaries that favor Republicans often weaken urban areas, especially in GOP-controlled states. This remains true despite the "one person, one vote" court rulings that mandate roughly equally populated legislative districts, and when urban authorities implement policies at odds with conservative preferences at the state level, legislatures dominated by nonurban interests often veto these decisions.

The controversy in North Carolina over a law requiring transgender people to use the bathroom matching their assigned sex at birth stemmed from the state legislature overriding the wishes of Charlotte.

Conservative legislatures have further tilted the electoral playing field with measures that make it harder for African Americans, Latinos, and young people to vote. Trump's claims of massive voter fraud are ironic given that there is no evidence to support them, even as the evidence mounts that voter ID laws and other efforts to make voting more difficult discriminate against Democratic-leaning groups. An increasingly diverse and metropolitan nation will end up with less-representative governments. (Dionne: GOP find new way to restrict voting.) https://www.clarionledger.com/story/opinion/2015/08/21/ Dionne-gop-find-new-way-restrict-voting

Texas recently added 5 seats to the house through gerrymandering and many states have responded in kind.

Extremism, Terrorism, and the GOP

Bullying was not generally considered a strategy in modern American history. Insanity was not either.

Trump's victories were the natural result of a shift toward extreme Republicanism and conservatism over recent decades. Looking back a few years, after serving 14 years, Eric Cantor's 2014 loss as a significant political figure was a sign of how the party leadership's alignment with extremism would backfire. Trump is more than just a product of his self-promotion skills, more than a fluke of the electoral system, and more than a beneficiary of unprecedented interference by a hostile foreign power like Russia or an FBI director who announced an investigation into Clinton. His success also reflects the radicalization of the Republican primary and the party leadership's willingness to foster resentment, conspiracy theories, and demonize opponents and the media. In my experience, demonizing has always been a political tradition in the Midwest. Republican leaders created their own mess—they built the environment for a candidate like Trump and then lost control over what they had helped produce.

Radical extremists have taken control of the Republican Party, and if they get their way, American greatness will become just a distant memory. The America they envision isn't the land of the free and the home of the brave that my ancestors dreamed of and nearly earned. The America these radical "burn it to the ground" types desire isn't the one that millions of soldiers fought and died to preserve and defend. The America the MAGA Republicans want isn't a return to some non-existent "Great Again" utopia of white-only citizens. They want a country built solely on their perceptions of the good old days. They talk about making this a "Christian nation," even though the Constitution explicitly forbids that. They claim to protect the children but have no plan to shield those children from school shootings, only from all those Democrat pedophiles who drink baby blood (see QAnon conspiracy theories).

They claim they want America to be a true land of freedom. But only if it is a freedom *from* accepting different lifestyles.

The civil war then and now

J. Michael Luttig, a highly respected conservative retired federal judge and key advisor to former Vice President Mike Pence, stated that "there is no Republican Party" and that former President Donald Trump is "a clear and present danger to the United States," even more dangerous than he was after the 2020 election. Our country's divide between Democracy and MAGA confederates is just an extension of the civil war. Racism, no matter how well hidden and dog-whistled (past the graveyard, I might add), forms a large part of the Confederate side of American politics. There is no longer a clear geographical boundary or a north/south split; now, it's simply a red vote versus a blue vote indicator. Regardless of who won the Civil War, or "the War Between the States," as they call it in the South, you can visit those southern states and, until recently, see public symbols of the Confederate military—flags, statues of generals, rampant racism, old war cannons on lawns, and even Confederate weapons in private collections. A common saying is "The South will rise again," which I often hear from a relative with roots in the Deep South. Jim Crow laws symbolized the South's ongoing struggle in a disguised way.

The actual U.S. Civil War left the South in poverty and filled with resentment toward the U.S. North, or the Union, which, in theory, won the war. The Jim Crow laws and lynching show that the South continued to be the South, showing little regard for laws based on Northern ideals of freedom. This allowed the South to maintain its identity through racism, flags, local heroes, and statues until specific federal laws, such as civil rights laws, were passed. Slavery persisted long after the war ended. Now, the war has shifted into a culture of conflict, with ongoing violence threatening to escalate into greater danger and more violence.

Left in poverty after the abolition of slavery, resentment and vengeance still persist among MAGA voters, fueled by MAGA representatives in Congress and a former president known for inciting violence against his opponents. Trump is even preparing his judicial system to target anyone he disapproves of.

Fighting against the democratic principles embedded in

the laws and Constitution by suppressing the black vote through gerrymandering and similar tactics is common in this conflict. The "freedom caucus," members of the House, fuel that fight by spreading lies, conspiracy theories, and falsehoods to undermine democracy. Democracy isn't just about majority rule but also about the right to live and practice life freely as long as it doesn't infringe on others' freedoms. That's why the MAGA segment will probably vote for a rapist and a criminal regardless of their actions. The real issue is why Alabama legislators refused to change their gerrymandering to exclude black voters, even after the U.S. Supreme Court declared their actions unconstitutional. The Supreme Court also sent officials to ensure Alabama redrew district lines to include black voters.

Echoes of Conflict: The Modern 'Civil War' in American Politics

The political landscape in the United States today is marked by a deep and widespread division, similar in some ways to the rifts that fueled the American Civil War of the 1800s. While the 19th-century conflict centered on tangible, geographical, and human rights issues, today's divide is more ideological. Yet, it shows striking similarities in its intensity and the core values at stake. What are the parallels between the division among Trump supporters and liberal democracy advocates and the values that led to the historical Civil War?

The Values of the Historic Civil War

The American Civil War (1861-1865) was mainly a fight over state rights and slavery, although some historians see it as simply an economic conflict. Charles Beard argued the war was driven by economic interests between Northern Industrialists and Western Agrarians versus the Southern aristocracy. He reasoned that the cotton gin replaced enslaved workers, which undermined that argument.

However, historians say the Southern states, supporting the continuation and expansion of slavery, conflicted with the Northern states, where anti-slavery and pro-union sentiments were rising. This war was more than just a policy dispute; it was a battle over the moral direction of the nation, pitting those who saw slavery as an economic necessity against those who regarded it as a moral abomination.

Today, the United States faces a different yet equally significant divide. On one side are supporters of former President Donald Trump, who often endorse fascism, nationalism, traditional values, and a skepticism of globalism and liberal ideologies through authoritarian tactics. On the other side are advocates of liberal democracy, promoting progressive values, inclusivity, and a global outlook on issues like climate change and human rights. Although this modern conflict is mostly nonviolent for now, it is a "civil war" of ideologies, where the battlefield is the hearts and minds of the American people.

Parallels and Contrasts:

Moral Direction:

Then, according to modern-day historians, the Civil War was fought over the moral issue of slavery

Now, the current divide wrestles with the moral direction of America on issues like immigration, human rights, and the role of government in individual lives, with race being at the forefront of all of it. Thus, maga becomes "make America White again."

State vs. Federal Power:

Now, the debate often centers around the extent of federal government intervention in various aspects, from healthcare to education.

Economic Interests:

Then, Economic interests, particularly around agriculture and industry, were deeply entwined in the Civil War.

Now, economic disparities and globalization create tensions, with different views on trade policies and economic regulation.

Cultural Identity: The Civil War highlighted a cultural split between a rural South and an industrializing North. Today, a cultural divide exists between rural, often conservative areas, and urban, mostly liberal regions, with rural areas holding the greatest political influence.

Media and Propaganda:

Social media and news outlets often serve as echo chambers, exacerbating divisions and creating parallel realities.

Although the modern ideological divide in America isn't a war in the traditional sense, it represents a clash of values and visions for the nation's future similar to the moral and ideological battles of the Civil War. Just as the 19th-century conflict shaped the country's course, today's political split will surely impact the nation's path ahead.

Understanding these parallels is vital for navigating this modern "civil war" and working toward a resolution that upholds democratic principles and respects the diverse perspectives that make up the American fabric. That will not be the case if Trump wins the upcoming election (see project 2025).

Gimme Shelter revisited, LBJ civil rights and war, tyranny, death, destruction, and 1984

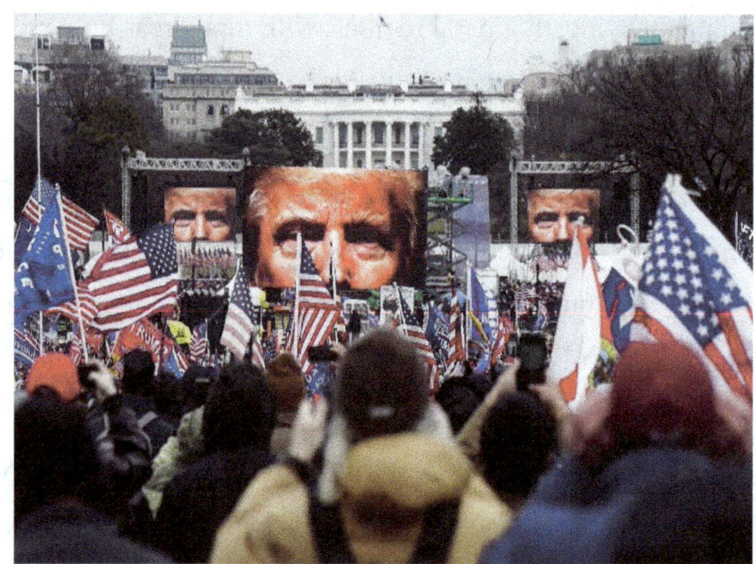

Stark contrasts defined the 1960s, embodying both great optimism and deep despair. This duality is clearly shown in The Rolling Stones' "Gimme Shelter," as discussed here, illustrating the turbulent spirit of that time. Meanwhile, the era saw significant progress in civil rights, mainly under Presidents JFK and Lyndon B. Johnson, who played key roles in advancing social justice despite their administrations' involvement in the Vietnam War and the country's struggles with political assassinations. The 2000s, so far, lack this kind of optimism. The anger, violence, and fear are now much greater, with no clear heroes, and the sense of doom is reinforced daily through widespread propaganda supporting fascism.

I am reminded of George Orwell's 1984. Orwell understood that totalitarianism begins with convincing people to believe absurdities—up is down, black is white, two plus two equals five instead of four, and gaslighting. These days, this translates to "slavery was good training for a job."

This quotation, which presents fundamentally contradictory statements, demonstrates how the totalitarian society in Orwell's novel changes the meanings of words to manipulate people's perception of the world around them.

Trump tells his followers that Biden is a dictator and that he, Trump, will save us from that. He claims Biden is running an unfair judicial system against Trump, the victim, and that Trump will save democracy from the Democrats. In his view, up is down, black is white, and reality is turned upside down.

We have large numbers of Trump supporters who are also members of QAnon, believing that JFK is not only one of them but alive and will soon meet them on Dealey Plaza in Dallas. Many evangelicals think all Democrats are drinking baby blood and are pedophiles. Trump's followers will believe anything they hear. We have the Trump cult believing in "Jew Lasers," that a South American leader, long dead, manipulated the voting machines in the 2020 American election, and that

Tom Hanks is running a kiddie porn operation out of a pizzeria. A majority of Republicans believe that election workers, other governments, and Democrats rigged the 2020 election, which Trump lost. Yet Trump's appointed election officials, Zar and AG, investigated that election and reported that it was one of the fairest ever. Election denial is "gaslighting" writ large.

Likewise, we have a Republican leader who claims that our media is "fake news," while the fabricated lies of Fox "News" are considered accurate. Supporters are buying into this, becoming the new Confederate Americans. Up is down, and Trump claims the threat to America comes from "within," as if pro-democracy Americans will be the downfall of the country and he alone will save it—1984 speaks. His cult, and that is what it is, insists we do not have a democracy; we have a "constitutional Republic," which, for MAGA supporters, essentially means a dictatorship that makes all decisions and eliminates elections. 1984 propaganda is effective. We are currently in a vulnerable, Gimme Shelter-like period in American history.

The 1960s, as reflected in the haunting strains of "Gimme Shelter," was an era of duality. It was a time when the shadows of war, violence, and assassination coexisted with a deep optimism shown in the progress made toward civil rights and social justice. This contrast of darkness and light defined the decade and left a lasting impact on the American consciousness, significantly shaping the nation's historical and cultural path.

Today, the darkness hangs heavy in America; little optimism is found. Sometimes violent and fatal demonstrations roiled the 1960s, the Vietnam War, and later the corrupt Nixon government intent on crushing the anti-establishment movement, all part of the moment and beyond. The country's political parties had radically different visions of America's future, yet cruelty was not the point. Ending democracy was never an issue nor entertained by any leaders. They would have been seen throughout our population as communists or unpatriotic. That would be an accurate label.

The same is happening today; there is no optimism or balance, and the cult does not see itself as communist or unpatriotic. In truth, it's 1984, with Trump and his MAGA cult labeling Democrats and liberals as communists and fascists; 2 plus 2 equals 7. Just as in the past, one group is becoming more radical, more willing to use extralegal measures, and more violent in pursuing its goals. Today, the Republican Party acts like a predatory faction. In a 2019 survey asking nearly two thousand experts to rate the world's political parties, the GOP was rated most similar to radical right, anti-democratic parties like Turkey's Justice and Development Party (AKP) and

Poland's Law and Justice Party (PiS). It is mainly based on ethnicity and religion. It supported a populist leader who pushed white nationalist policies at the expense of others, elevating personality over principle. The annual Conservative Political Action Conference (CPAC) in February 2021 featured a golden statue of Donald Trump; a poll showed 68 percent of attendees wanted Trump to run again, and 95 percent wanted the GOP to follow Trump's policies. The recent CPAC meeting also included a speech by Hungary's Viktor Mihály Orbán.

Republicans are now engaged in a desperate survival strategy, appealing to an increasingly rabid base to cling to their seats. This was most evident after the 2020 election, when Republican politicians openly supported or subtly approved Trump's claims of widespread fraud despite contrary evidence. Ted Cruz appeared on Fox News's Sunday Morning Futures with Maria Bartiromo to discuss voter fraud. On January 6, as Trump supporters cheered at the Ellipse, Republican senators Ted Cruz, Mike Braun, John Kennedy, Ron Johnson, Steve Daines, James Lankford, Marsha Blackburn, and Bill Hagerty made a final effort to overturn the election results. One hundred and thirty-nine Republican members of the House—66 percent—voted against certifying Joe Biden as president. Two House members—Mo Brooks from Alabama and Madison Cawthorn of North Carolina—had spoken at the Ellipse rally. It was James Madison and Alexander Hamilton's worst nightmare: democracy being dismantled by a faction's cynical power grab. Thomas Jefferson warned us long ago:

"The people cannot always be perfectly informed. The wrong part will be discontented; proportionate to the significance of the facts they misunderstand. If they stay silent under these misconceptions, it is lethargy, the precursor to the death of public liberty. ... Has there ever been a country in a century and a half without a rebellion? And what nation can protect its liberties if its leaders are not periodically reminded that their people hold onto a spirit of resistance? Let them take up arms. The solution is to correct them with facts, not to forgive and appease them. What does a few lives lost over a century or two matter? The tree of liberty must be periodically refreshed with the blood of patriots and tyrants. It is its natural fertilizer." (Thomas Jefferson)

We are fighting a new tyrant who has backing like LBJ never had. We need to fight this civil war of the day.

"Revolution is a spectator sport. The majority will sit in the stands and watch the factions fight. In the end, they will choose the side with the winning team. " (George Lincoln Rockwell)

Revolutionaries - true revolutionaries - are aggressive, ruthless, and quick to seize opportunities, as William Henry

Drayton did when he realized that stump-speaking was getting him nowhere. But defenders of the status quo tend to be cautious, legalistic, and hesitant to act until it's too late.

It's time to rid our democracy of the tyrants who have been growing for years, leading to Trump and the decline of democracy. It's the dirty part of the process and must be done. The underground weathermen of the 60s need to come back, not against the government, but for the government of Democracy.

The modern-day fascist extremists attacked the Capitol in January 2021. We need real revolutionaries like those in the colonies, and no king should be allowed. Democracy is the declaration of independence; We the People, not a dictator.

Will the war to save Democracy be fought in foreign wars or right here against maga terrorists in America?

We have an authoritarian who an American judge, Lewis A. Kaplan, describes as a rapist by legal definition and an indicted criminal who already tried to overthrow the American government and is now running successfully for President.

We have a Supreme Court with the will to overthrow the Constitution and take away freedoms that have been built over hundreds of years. Roe v. Wade.

Racism is central

Growing up in Nebraska during my first 18 years, I

knew black people existed, but I never encountered them. No school I attended from kindergarten through 12th grade had a black student. Even at the university, I didn't see any black students or staff, only white students, mostly of German immigrant descent. When I played with neighborhood kids, I saw a mix of class and social background, but they were all white like me, and race or skin color was never something we discussed in my family until the civil rights movement of the 1960s.

I played in a park in Lincoln, Nebraska, and swam in its pool, never seeing a Black person. I knew they were somewhere. People talked about Black people, mostly putting them down as a race, which always mystified me. How can you know enough about an entire race to believe they are inferior enough to make cruel jokes if you have never even seen one? It was white folks taking out their suffering on what might as well have been UFOs. I heard these people existed, but where were they? None of them were in my neighborhood. There were none in any of my friends' neighborhoods either. Someone told me they lived on "the other side of the tracks." Where were these tracks?

As a teen, the popular pastime before the mall was going downtown, hanging out, and maybe shopping. I never saw a black person downtown. I worked in construction, where the uneducated white trash and those who could otherwise not be hired for whatever reason worked, and no black people.

At a young age, around twelve or so, I heard the "Ballad of Emmet Till" on a radio station at Wesleyan University in Nebraska. I thought it was a story from ancient American history. It was a story from maybe a couple of years before I heard it, now a well-known lynching by most Americans, too gruesome to repeat.

My docile fraternity brothers from high-class families, who knew no one of another race, went ballistic with anger about the black people who did not exist in our town.

As a member of the father-as-professor class, I didn't hear much about Black people. However, the class itself was diverse in my neighborhood. Across the street, a kid I went to school with—maybe in sixth grade—lived in the basement of his house with his mother. His father was in prison. People in this small Midwestern town were openly racist, and the invisible Black person would sometimes be brought up to denigrate. I have seen historical photos of a Ku Klux Klan march down the main street of my town in Nebraska during the 1950s, a protest demonstration, I assume, against people I had never seen in that town.

Separate culture and language
I later understood why I hadn't seen or heard from

any African Americans; they were part of a different world and spoke a different language. When I moved to California, I found myself around Black people, and I couldn't understand anything they were saying. They had their own language.

William Melvin Kelly, the famous African-American writer and professor, wrote,

I would say there are two languages that African Americans created," he explained in one of his seminars. "One is being created so that African people can communicate with Europeans, and another language is being used for African people to communicate with each other.

This surprised me. The first time I heard the word "woke" was from a hard-right white politician, and it remains my only source. It seems to suggest an attitude similar to that of the political left. Using "woke"—a term that once described the "bleeding heart liberal" of the 1960s, those who care for others on a large scale, or political correctness—is now a way to criticize liberals. They are often seen as weak for not being as racist and tough. The idea of "tough" has taken on new meanings with the rise of politics that promote "cruelty as the point," as Mary Trump describes. While toughness might be an attribute in a combat zone, it makes little sense in society. It might make more sense in situations where resources are scarce or survival depends on oneself and family.

But the origin of "woke," according to Kelly, dates back to the 40s as a warning from the black community's language for others in the community to watch out for white people. It meant to be cautious in the South or around poor whites, as they often took their frustrations out on you with a rope and a tree.

By September 2016, the phrase "Black Lives Matter" was tweeted over 30 million times. The phrase "stay woke" grew in popularity and came to symbolize the movement and activism. Staying woke became the overarching goal for actions like #BlackLivesMatter (fighting racism), the #MeToo movement (fighting sexism and sexual misconduct), and the #NoBanNoWall movement (fighting for immigrants and refugees).

So "woke" is now the dog whistle of right-wing political extremists that is loud to the human ear. It represents racism and a call against leftist ideology, whatever it may be, whether understood or not, aware or unaware of what it entails.

For 219 years, every president was a white man. Almost every U.S. senator, representative, Supreme Court justice, and cabinet member was also involved. That the early founders had sanctioned mass genocide of Native Americans or that many of them were slaveholders were uncomfortable chapters in a mythic narrative of freedom and unbounded opportunity.

More dog whistles

States rights and big government is maga code, dog-whistle, for federal assistance — such as grants, SNAP benefits, unemployment, and health insurance. It also describes federal protections — such as regulation and civil rights. It claims the government is too big and too involved in the lives of "individuals."

Job Creators are people who own businesses that employ other people. For conservatives, this means rich people without saying that out loud. While 10% of the population controls 76% of the wealth, the last thing the Republicans and their wealthy donors need is even the slightest, burdensome tax increase.

School choice means students shouldn't be limited to attending schools in their local neighborhoods but should have the freedom to choose any school that meets their needs. For Republicans, school choice is a code word for segregation and allowing discrimination. It also signifies the privatization of public schools. Instead of federal funds going to public schools for teaching improvements or community learning, Republicans believe those funds are better used as vouchers, which can be applied toward private or charter school tuition.

The actual game: Invest in affordable property in an

under-served area, build a charter school on one of your properties, use public funds as vouchers to boost enrollment, buy supplies and services from companies connected to board members or donors, and hire and fire as you please without teacher's union involvement. Then, watch your investment grow over several years as the area is gentrified and your property values rise beyond your initial investment. So, desegregation is beneficial as long as we profit from it.

Activist Judges are judges, usually appointed by Democratic presidents, who uphold any law passed with a Democratic majority or rule against any law passed with a Republican majority. On the contrary, judges appointed by Republicans who support conservative laws or strike down liberal laws are referred to by conservatives as *"originalists"* or *"defenders of the Constitution."* It's cool if we do it. Just not you."

States' Rights/Leave it up to the states

This implies that states should have the freedom to enact discriminatory, racist laws without federal interference. Since it required executive orders, actual acts of Congress, and federal action to dismantle racist laws, conservatives justify their stance by citing terms like individual liberty, government overreach, or unconstitutional behavior. Essentially, they argue, "We don't think the government should tell you that you can't discriminate, so we'll leave it up to the states, which will turn a blind eye to protect your liberties, such as the right to discriminate."

Critical Race Theory is a code used to derail efforts to promote discussions about racial diversity, equity, and inclusion in public schools. Black students have complained about experiencing racism and microaggressions. By ignoring these complaints, the White parents attending school board meetings to send a dog whistle about CRT have shown that they believe their fears and resentments regarding a manufactured CRT controversy are more valid than Black students' actual grievances. -https://jehallen.com/2021/12/30/the-crt-dog-whistle

Illegal immigrants are Republican code words for undocumented aliens, referring mainly to Latinos and especially to Mexicans. – see History Network

Islamic terrorism is a term used to insult millions of Islamic Americans who see massacres with the same disgust as Christians, Jews, and others in the United States. "Radical Islamic terrorists" unfairly associate decent individuals and families with those who commit crimes against humanity.

America first claims that America's legal immigration system should be curtailed to those who can contribute not only economically but also demonstrate respect for this nation's culture and the rule of law. It calls for infrastructure that "reflects the architectural, engineering and aesthetic value that befits the progeny of European architecture." It states that public infrastructure "must be utilitarian as well as stunningly, classically beautiful, befitting a world power and source of freedom," specifically citing the example of the ancient Romans. - <u>MSN</u>

Real Americans is Code for white right-wing Christians.

Treating "evangelical White Christians" as a synonym for "right-wing conservatives" does no justice to the millions of evangelical white voters on the Christian Left or those who are not political." - HandWiki.

Minimum Wage - Code for "We aren't going to pay you a living wage "because of socialism." We are sending half the family to jail where they will work for even less. When we say "lazy minimum-wage workers," we aren't just talking about teenagers entering the workforce." - FactMyth

Tax Cuts.- Don't worry, we are going to cut welfare, but we'll also give you liberty and freedom from the welfare state. As you know, rich white people love creating jobs for poor black people. Just think about all the black people who have worked for white people in the past and how empowering it was." - FactMyth

Moochers and Takers. A moocher is someone on

welfare. If welfare isn't enough of a clue, let's add in a word that sounds suspiciously like the N-word. To this, I say, "Yes, genius, poor black people took everything. That is why they have so much. It couldn't be those whose wealth increases yearly who collect interest payments and profit off debt. Let's keep blaming black people." - FactMyth

Law and Order. Nixon, Reagan, and Trump have all called for "Law and Order." Are they trying to rally the base innocently? Did someone forget to tell them this is code for the N-word? We know they don't mean "Law and Order" on Wall Street or K Street. On which streets do they want Law and Order? Do they mean Law and Order as it was used to give "The United States the world's highest incarceration rate and (it) hosts more prison inmates than all other developed nations combined"

Anti-Semitism "Trump released a closing ad for his campaign repeating offending lines from that speech, this time illustrated with images of prominent Jews: financier George of power"), Fed Chair Janet Yellen (with the words "global special interests") and Goldman Sachs CEO Lloyd Blankfein (following the "global power structure" quote). The ad shows Hillary Clinton and says she partners "with these people who don't have your good in mind." – Washington Post

Shariah Law "Claims that brown Muslim people are infiltrating our country, so be afraid and vote for politicians who will support the right-wing... We first started hearing about this alleged threat to American justice in the wake of the Sept. 11 attacks, says López, when the Bush administration became intent on linking the war in Iraq to hijackers who were from Saudi Arabia. It claims that new brown immigrants are threatening the heartland," he says. "A prime example is Kansas prohibiting courts from drawing on Shariah law—it's not a threat. The point isn't the reality; it's the racial frame." – The Root

Illegal Alien "This phrase triggers fears about

immigrants as criminals, taking advantage of welfare and disrespecting the American way of life. However, somehow, the concerns are always pointed at the Mexican border instead of the one we share with Canada. "It's racial rhetoric about Latinos that is now being couched in this seemingly racially neutral language, and harnessed to support fear to get people to support conservative policies." - The Root.

Socialism: "We aren't going to pay you a living wage "because of socialism." We are sending half the family to jail where they will work for even less. When we say "lazy minimum-wage workers," we aren't just talking about teenagers entering the workforce." - FactMyth

The key is in the language.

The key is in the word code, such as "woke," which is not so much the meaning as the feeling, the feeling being hatred. Hate may or may not have direction or objects, but it is so convenient to have a word to bring up seething hatred for whatever. The coastal elites, black people, a beer brand, Porky Pig. Any port in a storm, any way to vent the anger of "I have to struggle and have very little" instead of "those who do not struggle and feel superior to me in education or class."

It is not only the white race that is dominant in America; it is the upper class that is dominant. And language is key.

Poor, uneducated speech as subconscious separation

Defining the term 'native English speaker' is complicated. The term generally refers to anyone who has spoken English as their first language since early childhood. However, many children grow up learning multiple languages at the same time — for example, if their parents are from different regions or a country has several official languages.

A certain perception exists around English that implies it comes from wealthy, predominantly white countries and is mainly monolingual. According to this narrow view, multilingual nations like Nigeria and Singapore have less "legitimate" and desirable forms of English, even though English is an official language in both. The most esteemed types of English are British, American, and Australian variants, says Sender Dovchin, a sociolinguist at Curtin University in Perth, Australia.

Within any country, some forms of English offer fewer benefits. For example, in the U.S., African-American English is often misunderstood and faces discrimination. Internationally, some speakers are judged based on perceptions of their nationality or race rather than their actual communication skills. "When English is spoken by some Europeans, including French, German, and Italian-accented English, they may be considered cute, sophisticated, stylish, and so forth," explains Dovchin. But she adds, English spoken by Asians, Africans, or Middle Easterners may be seen as challenging and unpleasant. In my experience, the latter is harder to understand because of the accent.

In the famous novel "The Hate U Give" by Angie Thomas, there are several instances where the protagonist,

Starr—a Black teenager who attends a predominantly white high school (Williamson) but lives in a predominantly Black community (Garden Heights)—describes how she navigates and negotiates her Black identity in a white space that expects her to perform whiteness, primarily through her language use. Although fictional, Thomas's depiction of Starr accurately captures the cultural conflict, labor, and exhaustion that many Black language speakers endure when code-switching; that is, they are constantly monitoring and policing their linguistic expressions and working through the linguistic double consciousness they experience due to having to alienate their cultural ways of being and knowing, their community, and their Blackness in favor of a white middle-class identity, thereby reducing discrimination. African-American young adult novels like "The Hate U Give" allow Black youth to see their racial and linguistic realities reflected in literature.

Black speech and Ebonics represent conscious or subconscious separation of tribe and race, thus fostering the "us" versus "them" aspect of racism.

The symbolism of words, language, and made-up politics is used as a code to represent "us" versus "them," as seen in QAnon, religion, MAGA lies as policy, and symbols like "wokeness."

America, I believe, has always had a significant MAGA

population, especially in the Midwest. It only took Trump to bring it to the forefront. I've heard them speak since I was a child in Nebraska. They were people who only knew a leader who was educated, civil, privileged, and white. When the leader is black, like Obama, MAGA supporters (formerly the Tea Party) respond by saying they want "their country back" (from the non-white guy). They became more outspoken when 45 became President, voicing everything they had been saying all along. Black people are the target of racist jokes in this group; white people are seen as superior, even if they are at the bottom of the class and caste system, compared to other races or nationalities. Racial discrimination is all lower-class whites have to feel in any way better than those at the bottom of society. And that has been the case since the start of the black/white divide in the Midwest, as long as I can remember.

When soldiers returned from WWII, white soldiers received free education and "no down" real estate, but Black soldiers did not. A century of Jim Crow and lynching persisted long after slaves were supposedly freed. Black and white people rarely mix, except for educated Black individuals who speak with white people in the language of the educated. The first Black President was highly educated and could outthink most whites. If and when the white/black dynamic unravels, MAGA may have a chance to disappear.

Its racism, stupid!

Much of the MAGA problem in America is rooted in racism, confederacy-style. George Wallace ran for President in the pivotal year of 1968 as a third-party candidate. He received 13% of the vote, with five Southern states primarily voting by white, blue-collar workers. He also gained many votes in the North.

Southern Republicans have considered themselves segregationists since before the Civil War and have remained so ever since — even today. Racism remains just as strong in much of the Midwest as it is in the South. When the South was mostly Democrat, they called themselves Dixiecrats, represented by Senator Strom Thurmond of South Carolina, a proud segregationist known for holding public office. In the North, they are openly Republican, and as Liz Cheney quickly learned after standing up to Trump, they are MAGA Republicans.

The following passage is from "The Everyday Language of White Racism" by Jane H. Hill. It recounts a story from the history of racism in the South at that time and symbolizes the ongoing racism still prevalent in right-wing politics in America.

This episode of moral panic engaged the most influential and prominent political writers in the national media. It gave us a good look at how their linguistic ideologies shape discourse about racism among White elites.

The majority leader of the Senate, a position Trent Lott held from 1998 to 2002, is the most important office in the U.S. legislative branch and one of the most powerful political roles worldwide. Lott was known for his strong ties to the conservative wing of the Republican Party. During a 100th birthday celebration in Washington, DC, on December 5, 2002, for Strom Thurmond, the oldest and longest-serving U.S. senator, famous for his longstanding support of racial segregation, Lott was among the leading national figures who spoke to wish him well. His remarks included the following 45 words.

I want to say this about my state: When Strom Thurmond ran for President, we voted for him. We're proud of it. And if the rest of the country had followed our lead, we wouldn't have had all these problems over all these years, either.

Lott referred to Thurmond's 1948 bid for the U.S. presidency as the candidate of the States' Rights Democrats, the so-called "Dixecrat" party.

The Dixiecrats separated from the national Democratic Party, walking out of its 1948 national convention when the Democrats adopted a platform plank supporting civil rights legislation. The Dixiecrat platform stated,

"We stand for the segregation of the races and the racial integrity of each race," and the party's slogan was "Segregation Forever."

Thurmond carried Louisiana, Alabama, his home state of South Carolina, and Lott's home state of Mississippi, securing over a million votes and 39 electoral votes—the most significant third-party showing in a U.S. presidential election in the past century. Although Lott's remarks were made in front of many journalists and televised by C-SPAN, major media coverage of the party didn't mention Lott's shocking statement. However, on the Internet, liberal blogger Joshua Micah Marshall quickly pointed out the racist nature of Lott's comments in his December 6 weblog entry in Talking Points Memo (Marshall 2002a). Marshall continued raising the issue over the next two weeks. On the conservative web, blogger Andrew Sullivan also immediately called Lott's statement racist. The first mainstream media figure to address Lott's speech was African American Gwen Ifill, moderator of the Friday evening PBS program Washington Week in Review. At the end of her half-hour broadcast on December 6, Ifill played the C-SPAN clip of Lott delivering his statement and, with a quizzical expression on her face, invited her audience to "Let me know what you think of that."

On Saturday, December 7, well inside the first section

on page A6, the *Washington Post* ran a negative comment on Lott's statement (Edsall 2002, Washington Post, a).

On Sunday, December 8, Lott's remarks became the focus of two major national television political discussion shows, CNN's Crossfire and NBC's Meet the Press. On Monday, December 9, Andrew Sullivan called Lott a "bigot" and a "racist" and demanded his resignation. On Tuesday, December 10, 2002, New York Times columnist Paul Krugman highlighted the themes that later became central to the debate. "Was Mr. Lott . . . ignorant of the aims of the 1948 Thurmond campaign?"

There was moral panic among the media when Lott's words became known throughout the country, and the tape was played for all to see how he mirrored the segregationist comments of Thurman.

Looking ahead to the campaign, the 45th President in U.S. history called for violence at his rallies and delivered hate-filled speeches. He campaigned not on policies, economic contributions, or citizen welfare, but on harshly criticizing his opponents, portraying the Democrats as enemies of the people, and labeling the media as such. Any opposition became his enemy and was used as a platform for attack. Party leaders stayed silent out of fear of his bullying. His bullying is quite juvenile, mocking opponents for not wearing a suit, being short, or calling a female candidate ugly.

Intimidation was effective, and racism became the accepted standard. When asked about the white supremacists marching and using violence against anti-racist protests, he said there are "fine people on both sides," adding a wave of the hand to emphasize to the journalists, "I know it, and you know it."

45-47 and the law

Currently, President 47 faces several indictments from four legal jurisdictions in the United States, all dropped when he became 47. Special Prosecutor Jack Smith investigated 45 and found evidence to indict him, but those cases were dismissed. Now Trump is directing his DOJ to "investigate" everyone involved in applying criminal laws against him.

As an update, the Supreme Court recently made several decisions indicating it acts more like a political body than an objective legal institution, with some rulings delaying most of Trump's trials until after his second term, if they are pursued at all, except for the Stormy payoff trial. Trump was found guilty in that case, making him a 34-count felon. The Supreme Court has also implied that a President has immunity for actions taken while in office.

Trump's company was found guilty of fraud and fined

$450 million, but the fine was later dropped. Trump himself was convicted of sexual assault and defamation, with the victim awarded $83 million. He is now officially a convicted felon.

Many of the "Freedom Caucus" House members may be guilty of insurrection, so it's in their interest to keep 47 free and in power to pardon them. He has pardoned all those involved in the January 6 insurrection.

This same 47th president has called for violence against prosecutors and judges, even going so far as to name those involved in the 2020 election vote count for his MAGA supporters to attack.

Trump criticized the press and the intelligence community, two groups in American society that traditionally provide verified facts essential for policy decisions. He prepared the way for undermining them by attacking both institutions throughout his presidential campaign and transition, often using his trademark sharp insults such as calling the press "the most dishonest humans" or "enemies of the people," and accusing the intelligence community of using Nazi tactics. These critiques targeted not just their work but their very legitimacy.

He believes there is a "deep state" within the government bureaucracy. He replaced some of the most skilled and talented people in leadership roles with "yes men," who are unqualified.

It is no secret that he has caused significant damage to the election process; to this day, he insists he won the 2020 election, but the claim that the election was "rigged" is false because 45 could not emotionally handle losing. There is now tremendous harm to that institution and the legal system. He might attempt another coup similar to what happened on 1/6. He is sending troops to blue cities in hopes of provoking rebellion by left-leaning protests.

What sane Republicans need to hear right now and up until Election Day in 2024 is that the Biden administration is not a dictatorship, as Trump claims it is, that the Trump trials are not an abuse by the American justice system of Trump as the victim, and that if Trump is convicted, justice will have been served. There is no need to hear this from Democrats and the media, but from strong Republicans like Chris Christie. Sane Republicans should listen to it from fellow Republicans they admire, such as Mitt Romney and Liz Cheney. Eventually, leading Republicans will have to show the courage to defend the justice system, even if it puts them in direct conflict with Trump and his supporters.

"Sometimes institutions are deprived of vitality and function, turned into a simulacrum of what they once were, so that they gird the new order rather than resisting it (What the Nazis called Gleichschaltung.) It took less than a year for the

new Nazi order to consolidate. By the end of 1933, Germany had become a one-party state in which all significant institutions had been humbled. That November, German authorities held parliamentary elections (without opposition) and a referendum (on an issue where the "correct" answer was already known) to confirm the new order. Some German Jews voted as the Nazi leaders wanted them to, *hoping that this gesture of loyalty would bind the new system to them.* That was a vain hope." (On Tyranny, T Snyder)

The four judicial districts that indicted Trump have been lenient with him, allowing him to attack judges, special prosecutors, and court employees. This sends a message to his supporters that the judicial system is corrupt, biased against him, and should be overthrown. Of course, this makes him appear as the victim, encouraging his supporters to support him or riot against the system on his behalf, even attacking judges and other officials, he mentions, ultimately aiming to put himself in control of those institutions.

The Solution, How to Save Democracy

1.Trump people are afraid to denounce this potential dictator for several reasons,

2. Fear of violence on their family or taking his cult away as a means of getting back in power

3. The hope of pardoning and chance (1/6), he will appoint them to a high office. His cult is the blind following of a dictator. Why do Republicans stay with him?

1. Loyalty: Some Republican primary voters remain loyal to Trump and continue to support him as their 2024 GOP presidential candidate.

2. Perceived Attacks: Some supporters believe that any legal critique or charge against Trump is invalid and a product of a conspiracy.

3. Dominance and Disagreement: A desire for their group to be dominant and disagreement with other candidates' views on specific issues can also play a role.

4. Character Traits: When asked whether they were backing him because of his position on the issues or character traits, 89% of his supporters in the 2024 Republican primary said it was because of the latter, supporting TMT.

Solution

"Most of the power of authoritarianism is freely given. In times like these, individuals think ahead about what a more repressive government will want, and then offer themselves without being asked. A citizen who adapts in this way is teaching power what it can do." (Timothy Snyder, On Tyranny,

2017.)

What do we do to save American democracy from becoming the realm of the strongman?

Trump is now the 47th President and getting his revenge while his "staff" implement Project 2025.

Frankenstein Protests

Democracy can't survive on its own; it needs active protection—through strong institutions, civic participation, and collective resistance. Effective resistance might be inspired by the classic sci-fi film Frankenstein. The image of villagers with pitchforks and torches confronting Frankenstein still offers an important lesson: when facing destructive power, communities must unite to contain and defeat it. Protest, often and in large numbers, is a sign of how to defeat fascism. After all, ***protests ended the Vietnam War, and they could be a way to topple authoritarian regimes***. The symbol of defeating the monster, chased by villagers with pitchforks and torches—as in the movie—might drive the monster back to the windmill, ending the national nightmare.

The New York Times reports that:

"a network of right-wing activists and allies of Donald Trump is quietly challenging thousands of voter registrations in critical presidential battleground states, an all-but-unnoticed effort that could have an impact in a close or contentious election."

"Calling themselves election investigators, the activists have pressed local officials in Michigan, Nevada, and Georgia to drop voters from the rolls en masse. They have at times targeted Democratic areas, relying on new data programs and novel legal theories to justify their push." Trump's Allies Ramp Up Campaign Targeting Voter Rolls."
www.nytimes.com/2024/03/03/us/

Republicans can't win on policy, so they try to disenfranchise predominantly minority voters who vote for Democrats. Americans must get out and vote en masse for a straight Democratic ticket in mid-term and 2028 elections to save our American democracy.

"The name of the game is driving and shaping the electorate in your favor and increasing turnout for your party," Bitecofer told me. Because that's the only way you win when representing a minority viewpoint.

I witnessed this firsthand during the 2018 elections, with the late frenzy over a "caravan of immigrants" heading toward America's southern border. It was a daily fearmongering tactic aimed at Democrats, with one simple goal: to increase Republican turnout in large red areas of states like Ohio, where voters were originally
unmotivated. And it worked." (Pepper, Saving Democracy, 2023)

One would think that the loss of democracy in the absence of strong blue voter turnout should be enough. But

Pepper points out strategy that works in election communication:

"Bitecofer calls it the "make shit popular" strategy, hoping to force the other side to act on issues that citizens widely support. And a common tactic accompanying this approach is to "make things as universally popular as possible by not branding them as partisan—we bleach all hint of partisanship out."

Make an issue non-partisan but held by all.

Notice when the Alabama Supreme Court ruled embryos created through in vitro fertilization (IVF) should be considered children. That decision brought universal denial of it as a legitimate decision, even by the "pro-life" Republicans, including Trump, as too extreme.

Participation

American democracy needs people passionate about protecting democracy and voting rights serving in the very positions where MAGA is trying to recruit election deniers. By taking on these roles, those who value democracy can protect it one voter, one precinct, and one election at a time.

While they vary based on what state you live in, here are some of the formal posts that we must populate with pro-democracy patriots: (Much of this material thanks to "Saving Democracy," David Pepper, 2023)

Poll workers: poll workers are essential to American

democracy. They perform various election day tasks to keep each precinct running smoothly and securely, guiding voters through the voting process. Their roles include poll judges or managers, who oversee the polling place, and clerks or workers, who staff the polling station. Poll workers are selected through different methods depending on the state; in some states, the process is nonpartisan, while in others, it is partisan.

Canvassing boards: in many states, organizations called canvassing boards certify election results. The political parties usually select members.

Election boards: in many states, election boards oversee and run elections, guided by state law and regulations. Typically, board members are appointed by party officials through established selection processes. In Ohio, each county's board has two members from each party—chosen by the respective county parties. In North Carolina, the process starts at the top—the two state parties appoint members to a state elections board, which then appoints four members (two from each party) to each county's board of elections from a list of recommended names submitted by the state parties. The governor appoints the chair of each county board.

Local or county election administrators, supervisors, and clerks: in some states, these positions are decided by election (either partisan or nonpartisan); in others, they are appointed by election boards or directly by political parties. When elections choose these roles, they can be low-profile events where a few hundred votes determine the winner. In 2021, in Pennsylvania, for example, many of these seats went unopposed, allowing election deniers to win simply by running or as write-in candidates. Under no circumstances should the operation of our elections be overseen by one side collecting participation trophies while the other side watches.

Vote-by-mail processing works: In some states, political parties have a direct role in accepting or rejecting mail-in ballots. In Texas, for instance, the respective parties appoint county-level Early Voting Ballot Boards and Signature Verification Committees.

Ballot adjudicators: a variety of processes and positions are used to adjudicate ballots that are in dispute due to mistakes, overvotes, misspellings, and other issues. In Georgia, for example, Vote Review Panels (comprised of representatives of the political parties and the election supervisor) adjudicate certain ballots to determine whether and how votes in question should be counted.

Of these formal election roles across the country, approximately 60 percent are partisan (political parties fill the roles); the rest are nonpartisan. In most states, it's a combination of the two.

We need champions of democracy to sign up for these roles for the long haul. We need trained and experienced advocates performing these functions every year, confident enough to stand *for* fair elections and stand up *to* whatever nonsense—planned or non-planned—may be thrown their

way. They also need to focus on the interests of the voters—willing to stand up for voters against an election bureaucracy that sometimes prioritizes cost-cutting or efficiency over voters' needs.

Citizens must ensure election results are certified as required by law. That's as important as public service gets.

Here are some roles to help make sure it happens:

Hotline volunteers: state and national Democratic parties operate voter hotlines to answer voter questions and troubleshoot issues that arise on election day or during early voting. The more volunteers there are to staff these hotlines, the smoother elections go.

Ballot observers and monitors: in many states, state and county parties appoint volunteers to oversee the opening, scanning, processing, and/or counting of ballots, as well as election recounts. These volunteers ensure that vote counting is conducted according to law and pay attention to issues such as chain of custody of ballots or, more relevant now than ever, potential disruptions to processing by other partisan observers.

Poll watchers are observers appointed by state or county parties (or sometimes candidates) to monitor in-person voting at polling places during early voting or on Election Day.

Ballot cure volunteers: especially in high-volume elections, thousands of voters often have their vote-by-mail ballots rejected due to technical issues like mismatched signatures or lack of ID, requiring them to take steps to "cure" the ballot for it to be counted. Similarly, some voters who submit a "provisional" ballot may need to provide ID or proof of residency to have their vote counted. These volunteers contact these voters and help them resolve the issues so their votes can be counted.

County or local election board liaisons: well before election day or early voting periods, local boards of elections make important decisions on various issues. Volunteers can play a vital role in observing these discussions and decisions by attending local election board meetings, overseeing election administration choices, and building relationships with local election officials.

This work can lead to advocacy and troubleshooting efforts before and during the election. Many of these roles are overseen by political parties, with some nonpartisan groups also involved. Regardless, as Republicans mobilize an army of election deniers to serve as poll watchers—and potentially intimidate voters or disrupt elections—it's vital that pro-democracy advocates step in to protect voters and push back. Check with your local party about how to get involved in these efforts. When you take on a volunteer or election administration role, remember a few key points.

1. Wherever you serve, you're making a difference. Anything you can do—even if it's just taking off work on election day to serve as a poll watcher—is important and helps to advance democracy.

2. Find the places with the greatest need—even if it requires sacrificing more of your time and comfort. Voter suppression and intimidation tactics are meant to disproportionately affect marginalized and vulnerable voters, including voters of color and those with disabilities. Look for chances to empower voters in these communities. For example, if you decide to serve as a poll worker or poll watcher, remember that the most needed location might not be the nearest polling place but one in an underserved community a bit further away. These communities are often more prone to poll worker shortages, long lines, poll closures, and voter suppression tactics. By traveling a little further and dedicating more time, you can increase your impact.

3. Don't wait for the November general election in an even numbered year to get involved. Primary elections and special or municipal elections can be great opportunities to learn the ropes and get comfortable in these important roles. Also,

protecting the vote can have a significant impact on the outcome of critical local elections, which are often decided by slim margins.

4. A dull day is a good day for democracy. Some people engage in voter protection work seeking some "action"—and they feel let down when everything is calm and running smoothly. It's worth celebrating when the lines to vote are short and voters can cast ballots without fear of intimidation. So wherever you participate, go in hoping for a dull day—and remember that simply being there and doing your part, you're playing an important role in protecting democracy. Your presence might even have contributed to making the day dull.

Local influence

"The parties that remade states and suppressed rivals were not omnipotent. They exploited a historic moment to make political life impossible for their opponents. Support the multiparty system and defend the rules of democratic elections. Vote in local and state elections while you can. ***Consider running for office***." (On Tyranny, Snyder)

Most *statehouses* rarely hear from everyday citizens. A staff member I once knew said:

"I saw how few people called our offices. Our phones would sit silent for hours. But I also saw how one person who got angry and called a lot could get something done because so few people contacted us. And when people did make noise, they often got what they wanted." (Anonymous local staffer)

State legislative offices are much smaller than those in Congress—typically, one or two staff members handle calls, emails, and messages. A savvy advocate can build personal relationships with those staffers (be polite), making them much more effective. Additionally, these politicians rarely face opposition back home or critical media coverage, if any at all, because local media has disappeared. This situation makes them very uncomfortable with public pushback. These representatives can be persuaded by the argument that if they accomplish what you ask, they would have reason to showcase it as an achievement in office.

Vote for sensible people who want educated individuals to be the ones making decisions for their kids. Elect rational candidates for school boards and local offices, not MAGA extremists, who aim to reshape America according to their vision of culture: white dominance, American cars, wife at home making dinner, missionary-style sex; America's history should not be dismissed as having no wrongs.

The reader might be wondering what they can do. The answer is what they did when things seemed like they were about to go over a cliff, such as during the Vietnam War—a matter of life and death. Become activists, organize and hold peaceful rallies and marches, and sign petitions. Push representatives, whether Republican or Democrat, with calls and emails, urging them to speak up and defend the Constitution while taking the opportunity to define what the Constitution means to Democracy. Call out political leaders, both state and local, and give them the courage to stand up, or your organization will see them lose their positions. Americans do these things when facing existential threats, and we are there.

Trump and The Constitution

Constitution:

A well regulated Militia, being necessary to the security of a free State, the right of the people to keep and bear Arms, shall not be infringed.

This amendment has been interpreted as a means of protecting individuals from harm by others. It also suggests protection against the state, preventing the removal of individual freedoms or non-democratic actions. It is important to understand when and how to apply it to different situations.

Education and Democracy

Harvard gets the message that America needs education about the history and benefits of American Democracy.

"The United States stands at a crossroads of peril and possibility. *We must rebuild our civic strength.* In response to urgent need, the 'Educating for American Democracy' (EAD) initiative brought division. There has been a widespread loss of confidence in, understanding, and appreciation for our form of government and civic together a national network of more than 300 scholars, classroom educators from every grade level, practitioners, and students from ideologically and demographically diverse backgrounds and roles, who pooled their expertise to create a strategy for providing excellent history and civic education to all students." (Harvard University, Education For American democracy, Center for Ethics, 2023).

Americans who grew up after WWII, when many soldiers died fighting for Democracy, are surprised by MAGA ideology. However, schools haven't focused on teaching the importance of Democracy over dictatorship, nor have they emphasized civic-mindedness in the past thirty years. (The Road To Unfreedom, Snyder, 2019).

In democracies, schools teach students that political participation is important. One "content standard" listed by the State of California's Department of Education encourages students to "understand the obligations of civic-mindedness, including voting, being informed on civic issues, volunteering and performing public service, and serving in the military or developing alternative service." The original public school movement in the U.S. focused on preparing students to participate in democracy. (C.A. Dept. of Education, Resources to Support Civic Engagement, 2023)

This emphasis is not unique to America. "School work is organized to develop democracy in school and consequently in society as a whole" (Sweden), "the Constitution states that a general aim of education is to produce good citizens, a democratic way of living and human solidarity" (Costa Rica), and "an education system that creates knowledgeable, democratic and patriotic citizens is the aim of the Indonesian government." (Glaeaser, Why Does Democracy Need Education? May 31 2007 Springer Science+Business Media, LLC 2007)

Update: Trump is not who voters are voting for.

If the American voter thinks back a few years, there are events and threats today that voters would not have taken seriously as they do today. One of those threats is the loss of American democracy, which is now considered a genuine threat.

An issue on our political front needs to be exposed, and everyone, including Maga, Democrats, Rinos, Independents, and Green Party, should take heed

Trump unleashed Project 2025 on inauguration day, which will bring major changes to the structure of our United States government. If you read Project 2025 carefully, the civil service is to be eliminated, aiming to rid the world of the dreaded "deep state" as invented by Steve Bannon, who is now out of prison. Implementing Project 2025 will dismiss the American government's intelligence agencies and all other civil experts. Once that part of the project is in effect, the entire government will be unrecognizable and disconnected from what it is now. All civil servants who are educated, tested, and experienced in their fields will be dismissed by Doge. Applications to replace them are available on the Heritage Foundation site. The key qualification for hiring is "proven" loyalty to Trump.

America and its government is in chaos, and the economy will be forced into shambles by tariffs and Fed tampering. Americans will look for relief. There will be some type of uprising from all walks of American life in the change and chaos. Trump will have no depth of leadership to remedy the situation, and no one on his loyal staff will either. What will Trump do? He has already asked Putin for advice on numerous occasions.

Trump will have Putin to look to for advice, and Putin will take the reins. The US and the West will be in Putin's control on a subtle or not-so-subtle arrangement. And that Putin is who the 2024 voters for Trump will have voted for. As Harris told him during their debate, Putin "will eat you for lunch."

Trump may be declining, but his staunch supporters are no less supportive. He never criticizes Putin; he only has good things to say about the "strongman." Why would Putin be putting forth the incredible effort to install Trump in the office of President again?

Remember that Trump went so far as to proclaim that he would disband NATO, thus leaving Europe open to Russian attack. Trump says he could end the war in Ukraine in a day, and it is true. He no doubt would declare the US no longer a supporter of Ukraine, draining that country of all munitions and help. Putin would quickly take Ukraine as Russian property. Putin would then be free to attack Poland and the Baltics. We know who Putin is, what he would do, and what power he craves from a historical perspective. Putin would conquer Europe with force through his military and then move on to the West. He wants the US to lose its democracy. And if it does, he will have his lackey in the white house who will believe he is in charge.

To wit: the great Helenski meeting of 2018 and trumps last failed war in Ukraine meeting. where Trump and Putin met with no record of what was said, and Trump seized the recorder-interpreters notes and most likely destroyed them. The after-meeting press conference said it all. Putin came out with a wry smile, and Trump came forward sweating and looking down as though in despair in both meetings. He stood behind his podium after being told by his own highly skilled intelligence agencies informed him that Russia meddled in the 2016 presidential campaign. Then, when asked by a reporter if Russia had interfered, he said, "I don't see why they would have," to gasps by reporters present. He also said that the rough relations between Russia and the US were the fault of the US.

His performance was criticized by Maga, Republicans, Democrats, friends and foes alike. There were guesses over what was said in that two-hour meeting, which included an allude to a Russian-held Trump pee tape taken in a hotel while he was in Russia.

The people involved in Project 2025 want a guy who *happens* to be Trump to sign the document enabling them to execute the project once he is in office. Trump has no policies other than complaints about problems that hardly exist in real life. Crime, immigration, and inflation are down compared to the trump years, yet Maga holds on to these long-gone problems from his belief.

Trans, pedophilia, drag queens, and classic books are not policies that ordinary people get anxious about in daily life or lose sleep over. I would add that those most concerned with these items may be participants. The elevation of these items to presidential-level election policies is plain weird yet these are the items cited in Project 2025 for taking control of America.

We are getting up-front information about how Trump's people will rule America once he is in office. He, through them, proclaimed that he would jail anyone involved in past elections he deems "cheated" him by what they were engaged in, donors of his opposition, including lawyers, judges, and other professionals, really crazy stuff.

His speech is slurred. He drools, rambles, and seldom spins his words into anything cohesive. The press uses language to make sense of these utterances, and the media always translates what they believe he might be saying. The greatest of his recent verbal accomplishments was "childcare is childcare" - the rest of that answer to the question made no sense. He again tried to make an issue of another "bananas" right-wing issue by saying: "Can you imagine you're a parent and your son leaves the house, and you say, Jimmy, I love you so much, go have a good day at school, and your son comes back with a brutal trans-sexual operation. Can you even imagine this? What the hell is wrong with our country?"

Trump's suggestion that schools are performing surgery on students demonstrates his deterioration of mind. School medical operations are not a thing that happens. Believing it is a form of cultural insanity. I would venture into the fact that no teacher or headmaster in our public schools has an MD specializing in such surgery.

Why are his people, the same people who are overall unethical and criminal, having spent time in jail for their crimes, not calling his inability to communicate and run for office, influencing him to pull out of the race as Biden's people called him into question? The answer is that Trump's goons have a plan, as reflected by their writing in Project 2025, to rule America with an iron hand, and no one in the media or law is taking heed. And Putin is waiting for them to destroy their our government.

Harris stated hat if elected, the consequences of his election would be severe. I believe this is what she meant by that is what Project 2025 does but cannot say it out loud.

We see the author of the introduction of Project 2025, Kevin Roberts, a long-time Trump associate, who is one of several authors who will take control once Trump is in office. He resigned from his top position in the Heritage Foundation once his connection to Trump was exposed.

Trump, destined to be a figurehead dictator, will do the bidding of the author of this section of Project 2025. It is not Trump running; he can hardly spell his name or carry a sentence to its end.

The CIA, FBI, and top ten intelligence agencies are highly talented and efficient organizations we depend on to keep us out of trouble and secure. They will be fired and replaced by Trump loyalists.

What happened the day Trump took over on January 20 at noon in 2025?

Kevin D. Roberts is the head of this project and a close comrade of Trump. Roberts quit as head of the Heritage Foundation as Trump tried to distance himself from the radical Project 2025 document. Here is a quote by Robert's forward to that document.

"Today, America and the conservative movement are enduring an era of division and danger akin to the late 1970s. Now, as then, our political class has been discredited by wholesale dishonesty and corruption. Look at America under the ruling and cultural elite today: Inflation is ravaging family budgets, drug overdose deaths continue to escalate, and children suffer the toxic normalization of transgender-ism with drag queens and pornography invading their school libraries. Overseas, a totalitarian Communist dictatorship in Beijing is engaged in a strategic, cultural, and economic Cold War against America's interests, values, and people—all while globalist elites in Washington awaken only slowly to that growing threat.

Moreover, low-income communities are drowning in addiction and government dependence. Contemporary elites have even repurposed the worst ingredients of the 1970s "radical chic" to build the totalitarian cult known today as "The Great Awokening."

Roberts repeats in this quote what Harris's vice presidential candidate Walz was talking about when he called these right-winger issues "Weird." This quote has no objective referent to back any of it as a list of American problems, thanks to the "cultural elite," whoever they may be, and not many sane people lose sleep over any known dishonesty or corruption outside of the Trump criminal enterprise who include his indicted, convicted pals in jail and indicted.

Trump himself is a convicted felon as of this writing. The judge in his "sexual assault" case said it was rape by legal definition. Trump tried to overthrow the American government and is a miserable failure at everything he attempts. He has been indicted for his 1/6 attempt to overthrow the government, taking into account the new Supreme Court ruling that gives him immunity for official acts as President. He committed this crime while he was a candidate.

Inflation is under control enough that the Fed has already lowered rates. Drug overdose deaths continue, thanks to American drug corporations, some of which have their owners going to jail for pushing the addiction on America, as opposed to the supposed problem of the Mexican "rapists and murderers" bringing it across our borders. Transgenders are whoever, and I doubt many children are coming home from school having been operated on to trans them for surprised parents, as Trump surmised recently. Roberts complains about the communist dictatorship of China as a threat. At the same time, Trump plays personal footsie with communist dictators around the world, Xi, Kim Un of North Korea, (and their "love letters,") Victor Orban, Putin, who is leading Trump by his ear.

Project 2025 aims to eliminate the education department, altering the allocation of funds for education so that only the wealthy will have access to the best education. Closing down education will be done through the fear of transgender individuals, honest history may no longer taught (slavery taught the slaves useful skills), classic books will be burned, and drag Queens reading books to children will be halted. All while the bullet holes and slaughtered children with assault rifles are something Trump said to "just get over."

I quote:

……..As Trump utters the last phrase of the oath of office — 'so help me God' — the first phase of what Project 2025's authors call "the playbook" begins."

Yale professor HoSang continues, "First come the firings. Thousands of federal, nonpartisan civil servants—environmental and food safety regulators; authorities in disaster relief coordination; attorneys overseeing anti-discrimination policies in housing, education, and employment; medical and scientific researchers—receive immediate layoff notices…. Next come the roundups. As drafted by the MAGA nativist-in-chief Stephen Miller, a broad range of law enforcement, from the National Guard to state and local police, are deputized for a new deportation army."

After the firings and mass deportations, HoSang warns that MAGA Republicans will continue to implement other parts of Project 2025.

In the following months, the professor explains, other parts of the agenda unfold. Cuts in corporate taxes are so generous they would make the robber barons blush… Pornography is criminalized. The same goes for abortion rights, emergency contraception, and many reproductive health programs. Say goodbye to most public sector unions, labor organizing rights, and anti-poverty programs.

Trump's extremist plans would immediately destroy what's left of the economy, creating martial law and chaos, calling it Hoover 2.0 and worse.

Why is this being done?

In particular, Putin knows that American intelligence and government agencies are highly skilled and hard to infiltrate, and he cannot easily corrupt them, despite Trump's fascist howling about corruption. As Trump's followers take control and replace experienced government workers with unskilled ones, America becomes weaker from the inside out, like a sponge. They are easier to influence, just as Putin would want. Putin and other dictators see Trump as weak and ignorant and view 2025 as their opportunity to take over America, something Putin has wanted since he recognized Trump's ignorance. During their debate, Harris said that Putin would "eat you for lunch." Most observant Americans understand what she means, and I believe she is right.

Trump held a rally in Wisconsin, actually referencing a Justice Department announcement earlier in the week that it seized 32 web domains Russia has used for its influence campaigns.

The Justice Department seized these web domains and targeted RT employees, formerly known as Russia Today, a Russian state media outlet with English-language content. The indictment accused the employees of violating the Foreign Agents Registration Act and partnering with a conservative-leaning media company to help sow division in the US.

Trump has, in the past, cast doubt on the intelligence community's findings that Russia was attempting to influence

US elections, including during a meeting he had alongside Putin in 2018.

Deemed "Doppelganger," the DOJ Russian effort employed a mix of creating sites with slightly different web addresses that mimic US news outlets, including one appearing to be The Washington Post, and are plastered with pro-Russian narratives. It also created other media brands to funnel Russian content.

"As of noon today, we've seized those sites, rendered them inoperable, and made clear to the world what they are: Russian attempts to interfere in our elections and influence our society," FBI Director Christopher Wray said as Justice Department officials convened an Election Threats Task Force meeting. Wray was fired when Trump came to power and replace with a fellow who had no clue.

"When we learn that adversaries overseas are trying to hide who they are and where their propaganda is coming from as part of campaigns to sow discord deliberately, we're going to continue to do everything we can to expose their hidden hand and disrupt their efforts," Wray added.

The former Attorney General Merrick Garland stated that "President Vladimir Putin's inner circle" directed the influence campaign with the broader aims of boosting support for Russia's invasion of Ukraine and "securing Russia's preferred outcome in the election."

If I remember correctly, the Mueller report exposed and indicted specific individuals in high places from Russia who did meddle directly through the internet in matters of the 2016 presidential campaign, and officers of Trump's election campaign were making direct contact and even providing data to Russian operatives.

Invasion of Ukraine To the US?

"I said, 'You didn't pay, you're delinquent,'" Trump said. "No, I would not protect you. I would encourage them to do whatever the hell they want." – ABC News Feb 2024

The invasion of Ukraine marks Putin's first step in reestablishing the territories of the old USSR. If he captures Ukraine, his next possible targets could be Poland and the Baltics. What could he do next? If Trump is president, he might dismantle NATO on Putin's behalf, enabling Putin to do "whatever the hell they want," as Trump has said. If that occurs, Putin could try to reclaim a large part of Europe. It makes sense that after installing Trump in America—who would then be protected by a loose coalition of Trump loyalists—his next move might be to expand Russia's borders to include parts of the West, starting with Trump granting him Alaska. If that sounds impossible, I challenge you to remember a few years back and imagine how unlikely it seemed that the U.S. could become a dictatorship with one man wielding total immunity from the law, as granted by the US Supreme Court, for any terrible decision he chooses—such as jailing anyone, including professionals like lawyers, or imprisoning opponents for long periods. If that is possible, then Putin could "eat Trump for lunch" and become the next strongman over America.

Note that the Supreme Court has granted Trump immunity as President. America has become a weak and disorganized collection of scattered actions, leading to an inwardly disconnected state waiting to be taken over by Putin or terrorists. Americans pretend that everything will be fine and will sort itself out. The threat is greater than any such hope. Project 2025 must be countered by not voting for Trump in the midterm elections before it becomes a reality. Let us stop pretending there is no threat. We are witnessing the end of democracy, which must not happen.

Appendix

Drawing from the Declaration of Independence

Twenty-seven truths about America, our Democracy and Rule of Law, and our rights, freedoms, and liberties.

In America, the rule of law is king.

Let a day be solemnly set apart for proclaiming the charter; let it be brought forth placed on the divine law, the word of God; let a crown be placed thereon, by which the world may know, that so far as we approve of monarchy, that in America the law is king. For as in absolute governments the king is law, so in free countries the law ought to be king; and there ought to be no other. But lest any ill use should afterwards arise, let the crown at the conclusion of the ceremony be demolished, and scattered among the people whose right it is. — Thomas Paine, 1776

America is now or will soon experience the experience that comes with a king, a fascist leader, and MAGA.

"We the People" hold to be self-evident these 27 truths about freedom—and about tyranny that comes with this experience, as stated in the Declaration Of Independence.

— All persons are endowed with certain rights, liberties, and freedoms that are unalienable and that are the bulwark against tyranny by government.

 For, "We hold these truths to be self-evident, that all men are created equal, that their Creator endows them with certain unalienable Rights, that among these are Life, Liberty, and the pursuit of Happiness."

— Government should secure, protect, and preserve our unalienable rights, liberties, and freedoms.

For, the King "has abdicated Government here, by declaring us out of his Protection."

— Government is instituted and its powers derived from the consent of we, the governed, in order that government will secure, protect, and preserve our rights, liberties, and freedoms.

For, "To secure these rights, Governments are instituted among Men, deriving their just powers from the consent of the governed" and "whenever any Form of Government becomes destructive of these ends, it is the Right of the People to alter or to abolish it" and "to institute new Government... laying its foundation on such principles and organizing its powers in such form, as to them shall seem most likely to affect their Safety and Happiness."

— Government power is limited, and government is obligated to conform its every act to the requirements of law, which acknowledges our creation as equals and enshrines our equal and unalienable rights, liberties, and freedoms.

For, the King gave "his Assent to their Acts of pretended

Legislation taking away our Charters, abolishing our most valuable Laws, and altering fundamentally the Forms of our Governments."

— Every person's rights, liberties, and freedoms—along with the rights of both the majority and minority—are best protected through the separation of powers among the Legislature, the Executive, and the Judiciary. By keeping the powers of each branch distinct from the others, the powers of all three coequal branches are limited, checked, and balanced by one another.

For, the King "has called together legislative bodies at places unusual, uncomfortable, and distant from the depository of their public Records, for the sole purpose of fatiguing them into compliance with his measures," he "has erected a multitude of New Offices, and sent hither swarms of Officers to harass our people, and eat out their substance," and he "has obstructed the Administration of Justice, by refusing his Assent to Laws for establishing Judiciary powers."

— Each, the Legislature, the Executive, and the Judiciary should exercise only the powers respectively enumerated and conferred upon it by the Constitution or otherwise by law, thereby both avoiding and guarding against encroachment upon the powers of the other two branches of government.

For, the King "has dissolved Representative Houses repeatedly, for opposing with manly firmness his invasions on the rights of the people. He has refused for a long time, after such dissolutions, to cause others to be elected; whereby the Legislative powers, incapable of annihilation, have returned to the people at large for their exercise; the state remaining in the meantime exposed to all the dangers of invasion from without, and convulsions within." He also "has kept among us, in times of peace, standing armies without the consent of our legislatures." The King "obstructed the administration of justice, by refusing his assent to laws for establishing judiciary powers," and "he has made judges dependent on his will alone, for the tenure of their offices, and the amount and payment of their salaries."

— Government should provide for the common defense, protect the homeland, support our allies abroad, and prevent foreign interference in the affairs of the nation.

For the King "abolished the free system of English laws in a neighboring province, establishing an arbitrary government there, and expanded its boundaries so as to make it both an example and a suitable tool for introducing the same absolute rule into these colonies."

— Government should wage war against foreign enemies only when authorized by the Congress of the United States in a Declaration of War.

For, the King "has kept among us, in times of peace, Standing Armies without the Consent of our legislatures."

— Government should only wage war against foreign enemies, not misperceived domestic enemies. The people are not the enemy of the government. Rather, the government that regards the people as its enemy is itself the enemy of the people.

For, the King "has excited domestic insurrections amongst us" and "has abdicated Government here . . . by waging War against us." The King "is at this time transporting large Armies of foreign Mercenaries to compleat the works of death, desolation and tyranny, already begun with circumstances of Cruelty & perfidy scarcely paralleled in the most barbarous ages, and totally unworthy the Head of a civilized nation."

— The government should respect the need for the separation of military from civil authority and the need to limit the military to military purposes and not to civil purposes.

For, the King "has affected to render the Military independent of and superior to the Civil power."

— Government should respect that America is a nation of immigrants from foreign lands.

For, "We have reminded them of the circumstances of our emigration and settlement here" yet the King "endeavoured to prevent the population of these States; for that purpose obstructing the Laws for Naturalization of Foreigners; refusing to pass others to encourage their migrations hither and raising the conditions of new Appropriations of Lands."

— Government should respect the need for free and open trade with the world.

For, the King has "given his Assent to their Acts of pretended Legislation: For cutting off our Trade with all parts of the world."

— Every person should have the right to petition government

and petition the government for redress of oppressions without government answer of injury.

"For, in every stage of these oppressions, we have petitioned the King for redress in the most humble terms. Our repeated petitions have been answered only by repeated injury. A prince, whose character is thus marked by every act that may define a tyrant, is unfit to be the ruler of a free people."

— Every person should have the right to dissent from government and to protest government peacefully.

For, where tyranny and despotism demand allegiance to the tyrant and to uniformity, democracy and freedom from tyranny demand the opposite – allegiance to country and to differences among people and opinions. "When a long train of abuses and usurpations, pursuing invariably the same object evinces a design to reduce a People under absolute Despotism, it is their right, it is their duty, to throw off such Government, and to provide new Guards for their future security."

— Every person should have the right to speak freely and to associate freely with others without fear that government will punish them for the exercise of their right to speak and associate freely.

— No **person** should be deprived of life, liberty, or property without due process of law, the promise and guarantee against arbitrary government by tyrants, monarchs, and kings.

For, the King "abolished the free System of English Laws . . . and established therein an Arbitrary government."

— **Every person is equal under law**, enjoys the same privileges and protections of law, and is subject to the same constraints and penalties of law.

For, "**all men are created equal [and] are endowed by their Creator with certain unalienable Rights.**"

— **No person is above the law**. The law applies equally to all persons elected or appointed to serve the American people in their government as it does to all other persons, and all elected or appointed representatives of the people are accountable under law for their offenses against the people as every other person is accountable for their offenses.

"For as in absolute governments the king is law, so in free countries the law ought to be king; and there ought to be no other . . . Let a crown be placed thereon. . . . But lest any ill use should afterwards arise, let the crown at the conclusion of the ceremony be demolished, and scattered among the people whose right it is."

— No person elected or appointed to represent the people enjoys the royal prerogatives of a king. America was impelled to seek its separation and independence from the tyranny of a king.

For, the King "has combined with others to subject us to a jurisdiction foreign to our constitution, and unacknowledged by our laws; giving his Assent to their Acts of pretended Legislation: For suspending our own Legislatures, and declaring themselves invested with power to legislate for us in all cases whatsoever." The King "has abolished the free System of

English Laws in a neighbouring Province, establishing therein an Arbitrary government, and enlarging its Boundaries so as to render it at once an example and fit instrument for introducing the same absolute rule into these Colonies."

— Every person should be equally franchised as provided by the Constitution and able to vote freely for their representatives to government in free and fair elections.

For, the King "has forbidden his Governors to pass Laws of immediate and pressing importance" and "he has refused to pass other Laws . . . unless those people would relinquish the right of Representation in the Legislature, a right inestimable to them and formidable to tyrants only."

— Every candidate for elected public office should pledge to the American people that they will accept, respect, and honor, the will of the people expressed in the results of the people's free and fair elections and that they will honor the peaceful transfer of power from one office holder to the next.

For, we the people hold all power and "Governments are instituted among Men, deriving their just powers from the consent of the governed." We the people established government by law, instead of by men, in order that our representatives could not, like the king, subjugate us to their will. Our representatives are subjugated to our will by Constitution and Law. "Lest any ill use should afterwards arise, let the crown at the conclusion of the ceremony be demolished, and scattered among the people whose right it is."

— All persons should have access to independent courts of law to vindicate their rights and interests, and the courts of law should be neither political nor beholden to either the Legislature or Executive.

For, the King "obstructed the Administration of Justice, by refusing his Assent to Laws for establishing Judiciary powers" and he made Judges dependent on his Will alone, for the tenure of their offices, and the amount and payment of their salaries."

— All persons suspected and accused of criminal offense should be protected from government abuse by the Constitution's limitations on searches and seizures, due process, equal protection, the privilege against self-incrimination and by the prohibitions on selective and vindictive prosecutions, double jeopardy, and cruel and unusual punishments.

— No person should be tried for criminal offense except by jury of peers.

For, the King "deprived us in many cases, of the benefits of Trial by Jury."

— No person should be investigated or investigated and prosecuted for offenses against the nation except in **accordance with law**.

— No person should be investigated by the Executive on pretext or investigated and prosecuted by the Executive on pretext in revenge and retaliation for different opinion or politics from the Executive or for personal offense taken by the Executive.

For, the King "transported us beyond Seas to be tried for pretended offences" and "quartered large bodies of armed troops among us and protected them, by a mock Trial, from punishment for any Murders which they should commit on the Inhabitants of these States."

— All persons should have the right to counsel who is independent of the government and uninfluenced and uninfluenceable by the government, and whose highest responsibility in the representation of their client is to preserve, protect, and defend the Constitution against abuse by the government.

For, the King "tried us for pretended offences" and "protected . . . murderers by a mock Trial, from punishment."

(Drawn from an interpretation by **Judge J. Michael Luttig Jul 02, 2025, Telos News.)**

END

Harris was elected President

Trump won the election.

Harris did not lose the election. Trump himself said, "Musk knows those computers in the election, and he helped put me over the top."

Musk's Starlink was involved in the polls, and Trump was aware of it. Putin called in bomb threats at the right times and places to scare off the Harris voters. Putin also created a lot of fake videos for propaganda and fed them to the voters. Estimates suggest Harris won by about 12 million votes. A Russian official reportedly stated that Trump owes Putin his election, as reported in Newsweek.

Did Trump win?

"He journeyed to Pennsylvania, where he spent a month and a half campaigning for me in Pennsylvania, and he's a popular guy. He was very effective," Trump said. "And he knows those computers better than anybody. All those computers. Those vote-counting computers. And we ended up winning Pennsylvania like in a landslide. So it was pretty good, pretty good. So thank you to Elon."

On X, some users were convinced that Trump's comments were evidence of foul play. "This sounds like an affirmation that Elon stole the election for Trump," one wrote. "Is he insinuating that they cheated?" a second person asked. "Trump confesses to cheating by letting Musk rig the voting machines. But that's OK. Right?" another person said.

Trump's team did not immediately respond to a request for comment. (Kimmins, Mon, January 20, 2025)

Genya Coulter, senior election analyst for the OSET Institute, a nonprofit group focused on accurate, secure, and transparent elections, said she knew Starlink technology had been used to support election infrastructure in one place: Tulare County, California. Trump won Tulare County with approximately 60 percent of the vote.

Regarding claims about Russian hackers swaying election outcomes, Coulter said she was "less worried about Russian hackers affecting vote totals and significantly more concerned" with the deluge of incorrect election information that Russian-linked groups distributed online before the election and the bomb threats targeting election infrastructure that officials said were "of Russian origin".

Putin may have been involved. A Vladimir Putin aide has warned Donald Trump that he is "obliged" to fulfill the promises he made during his presidential campaign to bring peace to Ukraine.

The President-elect said repeatedly during his campaign to secure his return to the White House that he would put a stop to the more than two and a half years of war in Ukraine "within 24 hours."

Nikolai Patrushev, a member of the Russian president's inner circle and former Secretary of the Security Council, told the Russian newspaper Kommersant that Trump was duty-bound to act on his words.

Patrushev said: "To achieve success in the elections, Donald Trump relied on specific forces to which he has corresponding obligations. And as a responsible person, he will be obliged to fulfill them. "During the pre-election period, he made many statements to attract voters to his side, who ultimately voted against the destructive foreign and domestic policies pursued by the current U.S. presidential administration.

"But the election campaign is over, and in January 2025, it will be time for the specific actions of the elected president. It is known that election promises in the United States can often diverge from subsequent actions." (King, November 13, 2024)

Summary, bomb threats during election

1. At least two polling sites in Georgia briefly evacuated

2. FBI says Michigan, Arizona and Wisconsin also targeted

3. FBI says many hoax threats appear to come from Russian email domains

4. Russia denies election interference

ATLANTA, Nov 5 (Reuters) - Hoax bomb threats, many of which appeared to originate from Russian email domains, were directed on Tuesday at polling locations in five battleground states - Georgia, Michigan, Arizona, Wisconsin, and Pennsylvania - as Election Day voting was underway, the FBI said.

"None of the threats have been determined to be credible

thus far," the FBI said in a statement, adding that election integrity was among the bureau's highest priorities.

At least two polling sites targeted by the hoax bomb threats in Georgia were briefly evacuated.

The two locations, both in Fulton County, reopened after about 30 minutes, officials said, and the county was seeking a court order to extend the locations' voting hours past the statewide 7 p.m. deadline.

Georgia's secretary of state, Brad Raffensperger, a Republican, blamed Russian interference for the Election Day bomb hoaxes.

"They're up to mischief, it seems. They don't want us to have a smooth, fair, and accurate election, and if they can get us to fight among ourselves, they can count that as a victory," Raffensperger told reporters.

Ann Jacobs, head of the Wisconsin Elections Commission, said fake bomb threats were sent to two polling locations in the state capital of Madison, but they did not disrupt voting.

A spokesperson for Jocelyn Benson, Michigan's Democratic secretary of state, said there had been reports of bomb threats at several polling locations, but none were credible.

Benson's office had been notified that the threats may be

tied to Russia, the spokesperson said.

An FBI official said Georgia received more than two dozen threats, most of which occurred in Fulton County, which encompasses much of Atlanta, a Democratic stronghold.

Police in DeKalb County, Georgia - another Democratic stronghold - later responded to bomb threats at eight locations, according to a county press release. Six of the locations were polling places and were evacuated. County officials were seeking an emergency order to extend the opening times at the voting sites.

DeKalb County police later said no bombs were found at the six voting sites.

A senior official in Raffensperger's office, speaking on condition of anonymity, said the Georgia bomb hoaxes were sent from email addresses that had been used by Russians trying to interfere in previous U.S. elections.

The threats were sent to U.S. media and polling locations, the official said. "It's a likelihood it's Russia," the official said.

Adrian Fontes, the Arizona secretary of state, a Democrat who is the chief election official in the swing state, said four fake bomb threats had been delivered to polling sites in Navajo County, located in the northeastern part of the state and which includes three Native American tribes.

"Vladimir Putin is being a prick," Fontes told Reuters.

A judge in Clearfield County, Pennsylvania, extended voting hours to 9:00 p.m. after a bomb threat at a vote-counting site disrupted the process.

Josh Shapiro, Pennsylvania's Democratic governor, said on Tuesday night that multiple bomb threats had been investigated and none were found to be credible. He did not mention Russia.

The phony bomb threats mark the latest in a string of examples of alleged interference by the Russians in the 2024 election.

On Nov. 1, U.S. intelligence officials warned that Russian actors manufactured a video that falsely depicted Haitians illegally casting ballots in Georgia. Intelligence officials also found that the Russians created a separate phony video that falsely accused someone associated with the Harris presidential ticket of taking a bribe from an entertainer. (By <u>Tim Reid</u> and <u>Sarah N. Lynch</u>

Max Dascu on "Substack" June 13

"The missing votes uncovered in Smart Elections' legal case in Rockland County, New York, are just the tip of the iceberg—an iceberg that extends across the swing states and into Texas.

On Monday, an investigator's story finally hit the news cycle: Pro V&V, one of only two federally accredited testing labs, approved sweeping last-minute updates to ES&S voting machines in the months leading up to the 2024 election—without independent testing, public disclosure, or full certification review.

These changes were labeled "de minimis"—a term meant for trivial tweaks. But they touched ballot scanners, altered reporting software, and modified audit files—yet were all rubber-stamped with no oversight.

That revelation is a shock to the public.

But for those who've been digging into the bizarre election data since November, this isn't the headline—it's the final piece to the puzzle. While Pro V&V was quietly updating equipment in plain sight, a parallel operation was unfolding behind the curtain—between tech giants and Donald Trump.

And it started with a long forgotten sale.

A Power Cord Becomes a Backdoor

In March 2021, Leonard Leo—the judicial kingmaker behind the modern conservative legal machine—sold a quiet Chicago company by the name of Tripp Lite for $1.65 billion. The buyer: Eaton Corporation, a global power infrastructure conglomerate that just happened to have a partnership with Peter Thiel's Palantir.

To most, Tripp Lite was just a hardware brand—battery backups, surge protectors, power strips. But in America's elections, Tripp Lite devices were something else entirely.

They are physically connected to ES&S central tabulators and Electionware servers, and Dominion tabulators and central servers across the country. And they aren't dumb devices. They are smart UPS units—programmable, updatable, and capable of communicating directly with the election system via USB, serial port, or Ethernet.

ES&S systems, including central tabulators and Electionware servers, rely on Tripp Lite UPS devices. ES&S's Electionware suite runs on Windows OS, which automatically trusts connected UPS hardware.

If Eaton pushed an update to those UPS units, it could have gained root-level access to the host tabulation environment—without ever modifying certified election software.

In Dominion's Democracy Suite 5.17, the drivers for these UPS units are listed as "optional"—meaning they can be updated remotely without triggering certification requirements or oversight. Optional means unregulated. Unregulated means invisible. And invisible means perfect for infiltration.

...

Enter the ballot scrubbing platform BallotProof. Co-created by Ethan Shaotran, a longtime employee of Elon Musk and current DOGE employee, BallotProof was pitched as a transparency solution—an app to "verify" scanned ballot images and support election integrity.

With Palantir's AI controlling the backend, and BallotProof cleaning the front, only one thing was missing: the signal to go live.

September 2024: Eaton and Musk Make It Official

Then came the final public breadcrumb:

In September 2024, Eaton formally partnered with Elon Musk.

The stated purpose? A vague, forward-looking collaboration focused on "grid resilience" and "next-generation communications."

But buried in the partnership documents was this line:

"Exploring integration with Starlink's emerging low-orbit DTC infrastructure for secure operational continuity."

The Activation: Starlink Goes Direct-to-Cell

That signal came on October 30, 2024—just days before the election, Musk activated 265 brand new low Earth orbit (LEO) V2 Mini satellites, each equipped with Direct-to-Cell (DTC) technology capable of processing, routing, and manipulating real-time data, including voting data, through his satellite network.

DTC doesn't require routers, towers, or a traditional SIM. It connects directly from satellite to any compatible device—including embedded modems in "air-gapped" voting systems, smart UPS units, or unsecured auxiliary hardware.

From that moment on:

- Commands could be sent from orbit

- Patch delivery became invisible to domestic monitors

- Compromised devices could be triggered remotely

This groundbreaking project that should have taken two-plus years to build, was completed in just under ten months.

Elon Musk boasts endlessly about everything he's launching, building, buying—or even just thinking about—whether it's real or not. But he pulls off one of the largest and fastest technological feats in modern day history… and says nothing? One might think that was kind of… "weird."

According to New York Times reporting, on October 5—just before Starlink's DTC activation—Musk texted a confidant:

"I'm feeling more optimistic after tonight. Tomorrow we unleash the anomaly in the matrix."

Then, an hour later:

"This isn't something on the chessboard, so they'll be quite surprised. 'Lasers' from space."

It read like a riddle. In hindsight, it was a blueprint.

...

The Outcome

Data that makes no statistical sense. A clean sweep in all seven swing states.

The fall of the Blue Wall. Eighty-eight counties flipped red—not one flipped blue.

Every victory landed just under the threshold that would trigger an automatic recount. Donald Trump outperformed expectations in down-ballot races with margins never before seen—while Kamala Harris simultaneously underperformed in those exact same areas.

If one were to accept these results at face value—Donald Trump, a 34-count convicted felon, supposedly outperformed Ronald Reagan. According to the co-founder of the Election Truth Alliance:

"These anomalies didn't happen nationwide. They didn't even happen across all voting methods—this just doesn't reflect human voting behavior."

They were concentrated.

Targeted.

Specific to swing states and Texas—and specific to Election Day voting.

And the supposed explanation? "Her policies were unpopular."

Let's think this through logically. We're supposed to believe that in all the battleground states, Democratic voters were so disillusioned by Vice President Harris's platform that they voted blue down ballot—but flipped to Trump at the top of the ticket?

Not in early voting.

Not by mail.

With exception to Nevada, only on Election Day.

And only after a certain threshold of ballots had been cast—where VP Harris's numbers begin to diverge from her own party, and Trump's suddenly begin to surge. As President Biden would say, "C'mon, man."

In the world of election data analysis, there's a term for that: vote-flipping algorithm....

And of course, Donald Trump himself: He spent a year telling his followers he didn't need their votes—at one point stating,

"...in four years, you don't have to vote again. We'll have it fixed so good, you're not gonna have to vote."

Readers may draw their own conclusions